THE
NORTH-WEST PASSAGE
AND THE FATE OF
SIR JOHN FRANKLIN

By

JAMES ALEXANDER BROWNE

First published in 1860

Read &' Co.

Copyright © 2021 Read & Co. History

This edition is published by Read & Co. History,
an imprint of Read & Co.

British Library Cataloguing-in-Publication Data
A catalogue record for this book is available
from the British Library.

Read & Co. is part of Read Books Ltd.
For more information visit
www.readandcobooks.co.uk

SIR JOHN FRANKLIN

By John Knox Laughton

Arctic explorer, the twelfth and youngest son of Willingham Franklin of Spilsby in Lincolnshire, was born on 16 April 1786. It had been intended to bring him up for the church, but a holiday visit to the seashore excited a strong desire to go to sea, which his father vainly endeavoured to overcome by sending him for a voyage in a merchant vessel as far as Lisbon. On his return he entered the royal navy on board the Polyphemus, then just sailing for the Baltic, where she played a leading part in the battle of Copenhagen. Two months later Franklin was appointed as a midshipman to the Investigator, under the command of his cousin, Matthew Flinders, and on the point of sailing for Australia. While in the Investigator Franklin distinguished himself by his remarkable aptitude for nautical and astronomical observations; he was employed at Sydney as assistant in a little observatory which Flinders established, and won the notice of Captain King, the governor, who used to address him familiarly as Mr. Tycho Brahe. When the ship's company was broken up after the wreck of the Porpoise, Franklin accompanied Lieutenant Fowler to China in the Rolla, and, taking a passage home in the East India Company's ship Earl Camden, was with Commodore Dance in his extraordinary engagement with Linois (15 Feb. 1804), on which occasion Fowler commanded on the lower deck and Franklin took charge of the signals. On arriving in England Franklin was appointed to the Bellerophon, in which he was present in the battle of Trafalgar, again having charge of the signals, and being one of the few on the Bellerophon's poop who escaped unhurt. Two years later he joined the Bedford, and, continuing in her after his promotion to lieutenant's rank (11 Feb. 1808), was employed on the home station till the peace in 1814, when the ship was ordered to North America, to form part of the expedition against New Orleans. In a boat attack on some gunboats in Lac Borgne Franklin was slightly wounded; and he had besides a full share in the laborious duties of the campaign. Its failure may account for the fact that no attention was paid to the strong recommendation of Sir John Lambert, in command of the troops with which he had been serving, and that he remained a lieutenant, serving on board the Forth frigate, with Sir William Bolton, Nelson's nephew. With Franklin's appointment in January 1818 to command the hired brig Trent, fitting out to accompany Captain Buchan in the Dorothea, Franklin's career as an Arctic explorer commenced. Their instructions were to pass between Spitzbergen and Greenland, use their best endeavours to reach the pole, and thence, if possible, to shape a course direct for Behring's Straits. The two ships sailed on 25 April, sighted Spitzbergen on 26 May, and passed without difficulty along its western coast; they were then stopped by the ice, and, being driven into the pack on 30 July, the Dorothea received so much damage as to be in momentary danger of foundering. They got into Dane's Gat, where such repairs as were possible were executed, but it was still very doubtful whether she could live through the passage home, and further contact with the ice was clearly out of the question. Buchan's instructions fully authorised him in this contingency to move into the Trent and send the Dorothea home; but he was unwilling to appear to desert his shipmates in a time of great danger. The Dorothea's state was such as to forbid her being sent home unattended, and Franklin's request that he might be allowed to go on rendered the task of superseding him the more disagreeable. So Buchan judged rightly that his proper course was to take the Dorothea home, with the Trent in close attendance on her. They arrived in England on 22 Oct.

PREFACE.

The information contained in this little book was originally delivered as a Lecture, at the Soldier's Institute, Woolwich. Wishing, however, to produce in the minds of my friends, and others, a deeper interest in Arctic subjects, particularly the Fate of the Franklin Expedition, than a mere casual reader can possess, I have determined to publish it (with many additions) in order that it may be more extensively circulated, and, at the same time, be more fully understood by those who heard the Lecture, and whom I cannot sufficiently thank for the kind attention they then paid to me. The Lecture (as will be readily seen) was chiefly composed of extracts from the works of Arctic travellers, the principal of which are Sir Edward Parry's, Sir John Franklin's, Sir George Back's, and Sir Leopold M'Clintock's narratives, and a work by P. L. Simmonds, F.R.G.S., in which is given a condensed history of all the Polar Voyages of the present century. Newspapers and Periodicals have also been freely resorted to.

The undertaking (in which I have received numerous encouragements) is one altogether foreign to my profession; but the subject of it lies near my heart.

The possibility of a short route to Cathay,* by rounding the northern coast of America, was suggested by our forefathers in the 16th century, and it occupied their attention upwards of forty years. The idea sank into insignificance—almost into oblivion— during the 18th century, but was revived with great spirit at the commencement of the 19th, and persevered in for 32 years, when a passage, connecting the Atlantic and Pacific Oceans, was discovered; this, however, proved to be altogether useless, for even if a ship could have made the passage (which was very doubtful) it would have taken longer than the ordinary voyage round the Cape of Good Hope. Many valuable lives have been sacrificed, to say nothing of the enormous expenses incurred, in searching out the

* China.

new passage : at the termination of each unsuccessful enterprise, many persons declared it to be the will of the Almighty that it should not be known, and cried " *desist ;* " while others said, "*proceed* and *proceed again;* " God gave the earth to man for his use and knowledge, that He, the Creator of the Universe, might be glorified thereby; and it would show a distrust of His Holy Word to be discouraged by one or even by fifty failures.

At length a bold party of explorators was sent on this perilous undertaking, but never returned, and in searching for *them* the problem of centuries was solved.—Englishmen love to engage in enterprise, and, notwithstanding the many failures they have ever experienced, and the disasters they have often suffered for its sake, their efforts have, generally, in the end, been crowned with success; they would, therefore, seem to lack the spirit and courage of their ancestors were they not to continue that desire for the progress of discovery which so nobly characterized their forefathers for upwards of four centuries.

The NORTH-EAST PASSAGE, round the northern coasts of Europe and Asia, was attempted many years before that of the NORTH-WEST. The first fleet which sailed from England on that enterprise consisted of three vessels, under the command of the illustrious Sir Hugh Willoughby, who perished in a somewhat similar manner to the unfortunate mariners of our own time*.

There cannot, I apprehend, be a person, claiming the title of *Briton*, who can regard, unmoved, the fate of the Franklin Expedition. It is one of the most exciting, heart-rending, and yet most glorious events recorded in modern history. That 137 men, some of them old in suffering, should voluntarily leave their native land, knowing to some extent the climate they would have to endure and the many dangers they would, in all probability, have to encounter, for the purpose of adding one more *bright page* to the scientific history of their country, and that not one of them should remain to tell the tale how, in their last extremity, they nobly filled up that page, is a fact, not only glorious, but also melancholy. Although in our day we mourn their loss, their names will ever be honoured by posterity ; and their history will serve as an example to mariners of succeeding generations.

* See Appendix No. 2.

I would here express my gratitude to Mr. W. P. Snow*, an officer of the mercantile marine, who has served with distinction in the Arctic Regions, author of " *The Voyage of the ' Prince Albert' in Search of Sir John Franklin†*," " *A Two Year's Cruise in the South Seas†*," &c., for his kindness in furnishing me with some information which saved me considerable time and trouble; and also for presenting me with "A leaf of the Prayer-Book found with the skeletons in the boat," as a relic of the Franklin Expedition.

JAMES ALEX. BROWNE.

Woolwich, May, 1860.

---

* William Parker Snow—"a very able captain . . . . a man who, descended from father and grandsire in the Navy, was brought up at the Royal Naval School, Greenwich, as a King's boy—apprenticed seven years out of Liverpool, has navigated in every part of the globe; is a man of science, recognised as such by the Admiralty, and having had experience of hard service in the ' *Prince Albert*,' in which vessel he was second in command, when commissioned in search of Sir John Franklin."—*Voice of Pity*, September, 1854.

Mr. Snow—assisted by a noble Lady, a number of experienced Arctic officers, and some influential members of the Royal Geographical Society—is now engaged in fitting out an expedition to prosecute the search for further journals, records, or other traces of the Franklin Expedition. Those who may feel an interest on this subject, and inclined to aid him, will please forward their subscriptions to the banking-house of Biddulph, Cocks, and Co., 43, Charing Cross, to the credit of " Snow's Arctic Search Fund."

† Longman and Co.

PART I.

" It is the only thing in the world that is yet left undone; whereby a notable mind might be made famous and fortunate."—SIR MARTIN FROBISHER.

The North-West Passage—Early Attempts to Discover it—Voyages of Ross, Parry, Lyon, &c.—Life in the Arctic Regions—Esquimaux Music—Back—Dease and Simpson.

" One day, early in the month of June, 1576, when Greenwich was a Royal residence, three small ships lay moored in the river, opposite the Palace. A Queen of England stood at one of the windows, waving her hand in token of farewell to an officer standing upon the deck of the larger vessel. Nearly three hundred years afterwards (1853), when another Queen sat on the throne of Elizabeth, a naval officer, travelling with all haste from the north of our island, arrived at daybreak in London, and announced to the world that the North-West Passage had been discovered." *(a)*

It was to solve this long contested scientific question that the first mentioned officer (Sir Martin Frobisher) fitted out those three vessels—the *Gabriel*, the

(a) Memoirs of Sir E. Parry.

Michael, and a pinnace of ten tons,—which sailed from the Thames on the 8th June, 1576. After exploring different parts of the Arctic coast, he entered the strait which bears his name, and then returned to England, having accomplished nothing of the object for which he took his departure.

The next navigator who attempted to force the icy fastnesses of the North was John Davis,* who made two voyages for the purpose of ascertaining the *North-West Passage;* in the last of which, in 1587, sailing through that portion of water now known as Davis' Strait, he reached a point on the east coast of Green-land, named by him "Saunderson's Hope."

The next two celebrated Arctic navigators were Sir Henry Hudson and Baffin.

Hudson made three voyages, and in the last (1610) discovered the strait which is named after him, and, sailing through it, reached that Mediterranean of North America—Hudson's Bay. On first entering it he imagined he had accomplished his purpose, and sailed on, fully expecting to reach China or Japan. We can imagine his disappointment when he found his progress checked by the opposite shore.

William Baffin, though serving in the inferior capacity of a pilot, extended his researches beyond those of any of his predecessors. In 1616, he sailed round that portion of water for upwards of two

* There were other attempts made to discover a *North-West Passage* in the interval between those of Frobisher and Davis, but they are of minor importance.

centuries known as Baffin's Bay, but now (having been proved by Dr. Kane and others not to be a bay) called Baffin Sea. On all maps published prior to 1818, there is, in the centre of Baffin's Bay, a large island, called James's Island, which Baffin or some other early voyager must have imagined they saw, as none of the explorators of the present century have been fortunate enough to find it.

It is remarkable to notice the tragical deaths of all these early voyagers. Frobisher was killed in the assault of a fort, near Brest, in 1594; Davis was slain by some Japanese pirates, on the coast of Malacca, in 1605; Hudson was turned adrift by his crew, in 1611, and never afterwards heard of; and Baffin was killed at the siege of Kismis, in Persia, in 1622.

The 18th century is not remarkable for any particular voyages, made by order of the British Government, to discover the *North-West Passage*. The only one was that commanded by Captain Phipps (afterwards Lord Mulgrave), in 1773, which penetrated to between 80° and 81°, beyond Spitzbergen. Nelson, then a midshipman, took part in this expedition.

The Russians at various times attempted the passage of the Polar Seas—Deshnew, Behring, Tchitschagorf, and Von Wrangel, being the commanders; but, excepting Behring Strait (and that was first navigated by Captain Cook), they made no discoveries of consequence.

At the termination of the great European war, in 1815, the attention of scientific men in England was once more drawn to the question of the possibility of a *North-West* route to China and Japan, and enquiries were set on foot. Mr. Scoresby, and other whalers, well qualified from experience to speak authoritatively, reported that during the years 1816-17, the Arctic Seas were, comparatively speaking, so singularly unencumbered, as to be absolutely navigable in many parts hitherto completely ice-bound.

They also reported that whales of the North Pacific had been found in the North Atlantic, whereas the whales indigenous to those seas are of a different species and quality. Moreover, whales had been captured in the Pacific which had escaped the hunters of the Atlantic, with broken harpoons sticking in their flesh, and it was hardly possible to conceive that they had swam round Cape Horn, crossing and re-crossing the Equinoctial Line.

Accordingly, in 1818, at the instigation of Sir John Barrow and others, the Prince Regent signified his pleasure that an attempt should be made to find a passage by sea between the Atlantic and Pacific Oceans, and the Lords Commissioners of the Admiralty were pleased to fit out four vessels to proceed towards the North Pole: two, the *Isabella* and *Alexander*, under the command of Captain Ross and Lieutenant Parry, to proceed up Davis' Strait and Baffin's Bay, and then to turn to the westward, in the hope of being able to reach Behring's Strait; the other two, the *Dorothea* and *Trent*, under the command of Capt. Buchan and Lieut. Franklin, to proceed between Greenland and Spitzbergen, and seek a passage through an open polar sea, if such could be found in that direction.

Captain Ross' expedition, as far as the progress of discovery is concerned, was a failure. The latitude of various points erroneously marked by Baffin, was, however, corrected; some very valuable magnetic observations were made by Captain Sabine, Royal Artillery (who accompanied the expedition as astronomer); and a few new specimens in natural history were collected. They sailed round Baffin's Bay, and penetrated for a few miles into Lancaster Sound, when the commander (Ross) imagined he saw a range of mountains stretching from north to south; these he named the Croker Mountains, and returned home, and reported that " Lancaster Sound was a bay, affording no entrance into any western sea."

This assertion was greatly doubted by Lieutenant Parry, and other officers of the expedition, and the Admiralty determining to continue the progress of discovery appointed him to the command of a new expedition, consisting of the *Hecla* and *Griper*, which sailed in the following year. They left the Thames on the 11th May, and on the 4th August following, sailed through the imaginary Croker Mountains, Parry naming the water Barrow Strait, after Mr. Barrow of the Admiralty.

And here let me mention that to the late Sir John Barrow, F.R.S., we are mainly indebted for the advocacy and promotion of the several expeditions, and the investigations and enquiries set on foot in the present century. He, himself, in early life, visited the Spitzbergen seas as high as the 80th parallel, and he also travelled in China and the Cape of Good Hope with Lord Macartney. He published his " TRAVELS IN CHINA," which, at the time, was considered the most valuable account which had appeared of the Chinese. He also published a volume of his " TRAVELS IN SOUTH AFRICA." In 1814 he received the appointment of second secretary to the Admiralty, when his ardour in the pursuit of geographical knowledge and scientific discovery was soon evinced by the manner in which he endeavoured to serve his country in bringing before various governments the desirability of prosecuting voyages to the Arctic regions. These services were honourably noticed in various ways; and in 1835 he was created a baronet. He died in 1848, at the age of 76 years.

But to return to our narrative.

Parry persevered in his course as far as Leopold Island, when he found the ice extended in a compact body to the north, and therefore turned his vessels southward into the magnificent inlet now named Regent's Inlet. They sailed as far down as Cape Kater, and then returned to the north, this time discovering a narrow channel between the ice and the

land. On the 22nd August they discovered Beechy
Island,[1] Wellington Channel,[2] and Cornwallis Island;[3]
and on the 1st September reached the large and fine
island which Parry named Melville Island, after the
then First Lord of the Admiralty, having discovered
and passed a number of smaller islands to which he
gave the names of Griffith,[4] Lowther,[5] Young,[6] Davy,[7]
Garrett,[8] Bathurst,[9] and Byam Martin.[10]

On the 5th September Parry announced to his
crews that they had passed 110° W. longitude, by
which they became entitled to a reward of £5,000
granted by Order in Council to the first ship's company who should reach that meridian. To celebrate
the event, they named a cape in sight Bounty Cape.
Parry called the group of islands he had discovered,
the North Georgian Islands, after the King, (Geo. III,)
but this has since been changed to the Parry Islands.
On Sunday, 26th September, they were *comfortably*
frozen in, in a harbour which Parry named Winter
Harbour, on the south coast of Melville Island, with
little chance of escape for at least eight or nine months,
during three of which the sun would be absent from
them.

Parry immediately attended to the necessary

1. Named after Sir William Beechy, the celebrated portrait painter,
and his son Lieut. F. W. Beechy, who discovered it to be an island.
2. Named after the Duke of Wellington. 3. Admiral the Hon. Sir
William Cornwallis. 4. Rear Admiral Edward Griffiths, 5. Viscount
Lowther. 6. Dr. Thomas Young, Secretary to the Board of Longitude. 7. Sir Humphrey Davy. 8. Captain Henry Garrett, R.N.
9. Earl of Bathurst. 10. Sir Thomas Martin, Admiral of the Fleet.

arrangements for the continuance of good health and good spirits among the crews.

The following is a short sketch of their winter life: On Sundays, Divine service was regularly performed twice, and Captain Parry says:—

"The attention paid by the men to the observance of their religious duties, was such as to reflect upon them the highest credit, and tended in no small degree to the preservation of that regularity and good conduct for which, with very few exceptions, they were invariably distinguished."

In these regions the worship of God has always been cheerfully attended to by the sailors engaged in the various expeditions; the great and magnificent works they behold—in the sky, in the sea, and on the ice, causing them to feel how near they are to the presence of their Creator.

Mr. Snow, in his voyage of the *Prince Albert*, says:

" Prayer—honest prayer—is beyond everything invaluable to a seaman, especially to one engaged in the dangerous duties which he has to perform in the Arctic seas. That we should go out with a due regard to this important obligation to prayer and humble dependance upon God, was what every one might consider as a matter of course; but I am pleased to say that, in our case, the *of course* was never needed. Spontaneously our men called for prayer and a proper service."

Captain Parry and Lieutenant Liddon (the commander of the *Griper)* set up schools for the instruction of the seamen—and in those days poor men could seldom read or write—and on their arrival in England there was not one man, of either ships, who could not read well. A newspaper was also got up, entitled the *"Winter Chronicle and North Georgian Gazette,"* of which Captain Sabine was the editor. They also had theatrical performances once a fortnight, the first of which took place on the 5th November, 1819, *"Miss in her teens"* being the farce performed. It was something very unusual for performances to take place on a stage with the thermometer standing 27° below zero, as also it was for *actresses* to have beards and whiskers. On the 23rd December they performed *"The Mayor of Garratt,"* and an after-piece by Captain Parry, entitled, *"The North-West Passage; or, The Voyage Finished."*

In the summer of 1820 they travelled about various parts of Melville Island, and on the 7th June discovered a small island to the north-east which Parry named after his companion Captain Sabine; this, however, in 1851, was proved to be a part of Melville Island, and is therefore now called Sabine Peninsula. On their return journey to the ship the wheels of the cart were broken, which greatly increased the difficulties of travelling, as the provisions, &c., had to be divided among the men. These cart wheels were found by Commander McClintock in 1851, precisely as they were left by Parry in 1820; and being greatly in need of fire-wood, he used them for that purpose, bringing, however, the iron home as a trophy. Mr. Fisher, the surgeon of the *Hecla,* recorded the visit of the expedition to Melville Island on a sandstone rock in Winter Harbour, and the inscription was found to be quite legible when Captain Austin visited that spot in 1851. The ships left their winter quarters on the 1st August, but were not able to force a passage westward, and after sighting "Banks's Land," the expedition returned home, entering Baffin's Bay on the 5th September, and arriving in England on the 30th October.

At his own desire, a few months after his return, the Admiralty gave Parry the command of another expedition, with instructions to proceed through Hudson's Strait, and try and find an outlet from the bay into the Polar Sea. The ships engaged in this expedition were the *Fury* * and *Hecla,* Commander Lyon having charge of the latter. They sailed in May, 1821, and by October had proceeded no further than a small island in Fox Channel, where they were obliged to select winter quarters, and to which Parry gave the name of "Winter Isle."

An arctic winter was, by this time, no novelty to the crews of the *Fury* and *Hecla,* (most of whom had belonged to the *Hecla* and *Griper,* 1819-20) and the experience of Melville Island had taught Captain

---

* On the 17th April, 1821, previous to the departure of this expedition, a ball was given on board the *Fury;* the music being performed by the Royal Artillery Band.

Parry the best means to be employed for the preservation of health and comfort.

The theatrical performances of the last voyage were greatly improved upon, and occasionally varied by the exhibition of an excellent magic lantern, presented to the expedition by an unknown lady. Concerts were also added to the entertainments, and Parry, writing on the subject, says :—

"More skilful amateurs might have smiled at these our humble concerts; but it will not incline them to think less of the science they admire, to be assured that, in these remote and desolate regions of the globe, it has often furnished us with the most pleasurable sensations which our situation was capable of affording. Independently of the mere gratification to the ear, there is, perhaps, scarcely a person in the world really fond of music, in whose mind its sound is not, more or less, connected with his far distant home."

During this winter they were visited by a tribe of Esquimaux, who, in intellect, honesty, and appearance, were far superior to any of the tribes previously visited by Europeans.

Among other accomplishments, they were tolerable musicians, all things being considered. Captain Parry paid particular attention to their abilities in this branch of science, and noted down two of the songs he had the *inexpressible pleasure* of listening to. He says, "the women will go on singing for nearly half an hour, and then leave off one by one, not with their story, but their breath exhausted."

The following are the songs imported from Winter Isle by Captain Parry:—

The second is far more melodious; indeed Beethoven was not above writing a phrase in his Overture to Leonora which corresponds with four bars of it:—

While on the subject of Esquimaux music, I will give one more specimen, which was heard in Smith's Sound, by Dr. Kane, in 1854:—

As this is the music of that family of mankind residing nearest to the Pole, we must prize it accordingly.

Among the Esquimaux who visited the *Fury* and *Hecla*, was an interesting female, by name Iligliuk, who possessed a large fund of useful information. She had a good ear for music, a ready eye for everything, was an excellent sempstress, and had such a good idea of the hydrography and bearings of the neighbouring coasts as to draw charts which guided Parry in his future operations, and which he proved to be in the main correct.

The first land they approached after leaving Winter Isle (in the summer of 1822), was a small island that had been accurately described by the *fair* Esquimaux, and named by her Igloolik, which name it still retains. This year they only advanced forty miles westward of Igloolik, when they were frozen in for the second winter. The strait in which they were situated was named after the ships, the " Fury and Hecla Strait."

The following summer (1823), gave them no advantage, so on the 1st August, Captain Parry reluctantly gave orders for the return of the expedition.

In 1823, Captain Sabine, R.A., who had been for some time engaged in magnetic observations, and also in experiments to determine the configuration of the earth, by means of pendulum vibrations in different latitudes, having perfected his observations at different points, from the Equator to the Arctic Circle, suggested to the Royal Society, through Sir Humphrey Davy, the importance of extending similar experiments into higher latitudes towards the Pole. Accordingly, the Government placed at his disposal H.M.S. *Griper*, 123 tons, Commander Clavering, which was to convey him to Spitzbergen, and thence to the east coast of Greenland.

They sailed from the Thames on the 11th May, and in about three weeks reached Whale Island, near the North Cape, Norway. After staying here from the 4th to the 23rd June, they proceeded on their voyage, arriving at Spitzbergen in a few days. Capt. Sabine made his observations on one of the small islands round Hakluyt's Headland, Clavering, meanwhile, sailing due north, reached Lat. 80° 20′, where he was stopped by an impenetrable barrier of ice, and compelled to return. By the 24th July all were on board again, and the vessel's course was directed for the east coast of Greenland; and after some valuable observations were made by Sabine, they returned to England, arriving at Deptford on the 19th December.

The *Griper* had not been home many months when she was again commissioned for the purpose of Arctic discovery, and sailed for Melville Peninsula on the 20th June, 1824, under the command of Captain Lyon. She made but slow progress, and it was not until the end of August that she rounded the southern head of Southampton Island, and stood up towards Sir Thomas Roe's Welcome. On reaching the entrance of this channel they encountered a terrific gale, which for a long time threatened the destruction of both ship and crew. Drifting with this, they brought up the ship with four anchors, in a bay with five fathoms and a half water, in the momentary expectation that with the ebb tide the ship would take the ground, as the sea broke fearfully on a low sandy beach just astern, and had the anchors parted nothing could have saved the vessel. Neither commander nor crew had been in bed for three nights, and although little hope was entertained of surviving the gale, and no boat could live in such a sea, the officers and crew performed their several duties with their accustomed coolness. Each man was ordered to put on his warmest clothing, and to take charge of some useful instrument. The scene is best described in the words of the gallant commander :—

"Each, therefore, brought his bag on deck and dressed himself; and in the fine athletic forms which stood exposed before me, I did not see one muscle quiver, nor the slightest sign of alarm. Prayers were read, and they then all sat down in groups, sheltered from the wash of the sea by whatever they could find, and some endeavoured to obtain a little sleep. Never perhaps was witnessed a finer scene than on the deck of my little ship, when all hope of life had left us. Noble as the character of the British sailor is always allowed to be in cases of danger, yet I did not believe it to be possible that among forty-one persons not one repining word should have been uttered. Each was at peace with his neighbour and all the world ; and I am firmly persuaded that the resignation which was then shown to the will of the Almighty, was the means of obtaining His mercy. God was merciful to us, and the tide, almost miraculously, fell no lower." The appropriate name of the Bay of God's Mercy

was given to this spot by Captain Lyon. A month
later they encountered another fearful storm, which
so dreadfully crippled the ship, that it was unani-
mously resolved by the officers that it would be
madness to continue the voyage, and accordingly
their course was shaped for England.

In 1824, a bold and combined attempt was made to
discover the North-West Passage, three expeditions
being simultaneously engaged in various directions.

Captain Parry, with the *Hecla* and *Fury*, went the
old route, by Lancaster Sound ; Captain Beechey, in
the *Blossom*, by Behring's Strait, and Captain Franklin, by land, from Hudson's Bay to the shores of the
Polar Sea.* It is needless to state that notwithstanding the untiring efforts of these bold explorators,
they were unsuccessful. Parry proceeded no further
than the eastern side of North Somerset, in Regent's
Inlet, where, on a spot since called Fury Beach, the
Fury was totally wrecked. The whole of her stores
and provisions, however, were saved, and deposited on
the spot ; and they have proved of great value to
subsequent expeditions. This is one of the many
proofs that "all things work together for good, with
them that love the Lord," for had not the *Fury* been
wrecked in 1825, the crew of the *Victory* would have
perished in 1831 ; and the crew of the *Fox* would have
suffered for the want of sugar (an absolute necessity
in these regions), in 1859.

* A short account of Franklin's first land expedition will be found
at page 33.

Captain Beechey reached Point Barrow, where he was to have co-operated with Franklin, but they never met, though at one time Franklin's boats were only 160 miles from a party of the *Blossom* who was waiting for them.

Parry made a voyage in 1827 to try and reach the Pole, and though he did not accomplish his object, he " unfurled his country's flag at a higher latitude than any, before or since, have been able to reach." [1] " No successor on the path of Arctic adventure has yet snatched the chaplet from the brow of this great navigator. Parry is still the champion of the north." [2] As this was his last effort in the Arctic regions, it were indeed ungraceful to close the account of the *deeds* without passing a tribute to the *character* of this great Christian hero.

Few names are entitled to higher honour in the history of English seamanship, or of English Christianity, than that of Sir W. Edward Parry. As a seaman, he was bold, enterprising, and skilful; as a Christian, he was enlightened, devout, and active, without affectation and without gloom." [3] He disliked public balls, and held theatres in abhorrence, and yet he was fond of dancing and partial to plays. He knew, as an old writer quaintly observes :—" That as an art teaching mankind to move agreeably to the cadence of music, dancing is lawful and commendable ;

1. Rev. E. Parry. 2. *The Times*, 1856. 3. Biographical Tract.

c

but the practice of it in a mixed company, which exposes the dancers to a thousand disorders, is the only thing to blame, where it can only serve to corrupt the heart, and make a dangerous attack upon chastity." [4] He also knew that a good moral play not only afforded innocent amusement, but was often the means of improvement, and he frequently, even when an old man, took part in private theatricals; but the " habits of dissipation, and craving for excitement " produced by the regular attendance at a theatre, he knew was good for neither body nor soul. He was born at Bath in 1790, and died at Ems, in Germany, in July, 1855. His remains, however, were brought to England and interred in Greenwich Hospital. Parry and Franklin were inseparable friends, and each was a true type of the other, both in public and private life. Both were engaged in boat service during the American War of 1814; both started on their first Arctic voyage in 1818 (it was then their acquaintance commenced, which ripened into the unbroken friendship of kindred natures for nearly 40 years); they were both married twice; both resided for some years at the antipodes, Parry being Commissioner of Port Stephens (Australia), and Franklin, Governor of Tasmania; they were knighted together in 1829, and received an Oxford degree in

4. Universal Magazine, 1753.

the same year. On the latter occasion a prize poem, containing the following verse, was written :—

"But fairer England greets the wanderer now,
Unfading laurels shade her PARRY's brow ;
And on the proud memorials of her fame
Lives, linked with deathless glory, FRANKLIN's name."

Sir Edward used to say "his dear friend was in his sleeping as well as his waking thoughts," and among his most treasured memorials was found a paper with the following touching endorsement— "Dear Franklin's last letter to me, July 10th, 1845."

The next expedition was that of Sir John Ross, who, in 1829, went at the expense of Mr. Felix Booth, an eminent distiller, who nobly contributed £1,700 for that object which the Government had determined to spend no more money upon, viz., the solution of the long-agitated problem of the NORTH-WEST PASSAGE. They sailed from Woolwich in the *Victory*, on the 23rd May, 1829, and on the 18th June passed Malin Head, on the north-west coast of Ireland.

. . . .

Three years elapsed and this expedition had not returned, neither had any accounts of it been received. The friends of the missing navigators naturally became anxious for their safety, and in August, 1832, Mr. George Ross (brother of Sir John, and father of Commander, now Sir James Ross) presented a petition to the King, praying his Majesty's gracious sanction to the immediate dispatch of an expedition for rescuing, or, at least, ascertaining the fate of his

son and brother, and the party under their command;
and Captain Back was proposed as the leader.

The sanction having been obtained, and all the
arrangements made for this relief expedition, Captain
Back, Dr. King, and three men started from Liverpool on the 17th February, 1833, and, on arriving at
the Hudson's Bay territory, they were joined by Mr.
McLeod, four volunteers from the Royal Artillery,*

* The Royal Artillery has been represented in these regions on
several occasions. General Sabine served in three expeditions, and
in Sir John Ross' (1818), and Sir Edward Parry's (1819-20), he was
accompanied by a sergeant and a gunner. Sergeant Martin, who
served in Parry's first voyage, was of some service to the expedition
as a naturalist; and both he and Gunner Smith (Captain Sabine's
servant) are frequently honourably mentioned by Captain Parry.
On the 24th February, 1820, while they were in the Observatory at
Melville Island, a fire broke out which destroyed that building; and
they both greatly distinguished themselves in their attempts to subdue
the flames and save the magnetic instruments. Parry says:—John
Smith, of the Artillery, who was Captain Sabine's servant, and who,
together with Sergeant Martin, happened to be in the house at the
time the fire broke out, suffered most severely. In their anxiety
to save the dipping needle, which was standing close to the stove,
and of which they knew the value, they immediately ran out with it;
and Smith not having time to put on his gloves, had his fingers in
half an hour so benumbed, and the animation so completely suspended,
that on his being taken on board by Mr. Edwards, and having his
hands plunged into a basin of cold water, the surface of the water was
immediately frozen by the intense cold thus suddenly communicated
to it; and notwithstanding the most humane and unremitting attention
paid him by the medical gentlemen, it was found necessary, some time
after to resort to the amputation of a part of four fingers on the one
hand and three on the other."

The men who accompanied this expedition of Sir George Back,
were *John Ross, William Malley, Hugh Carron,* and *David Williamson.*
The latter was discharged on account of ill-health, and afterwards
died: the following extracts will show Captain Back's anxiety con-

some of the Hudson's Bay sailors, and a party of Canadians, in all 27 persons. The expedition, which was to proceed overland to the Polar Sea, commenced

cerning him : – "The serious apprehension raised in my mind about the fate of David Williamson, the artilleryman, who had been so lately discharged, was infinitely worse. It appeared that he had left the fishery with his companions, and two Indians as guides; but, being a slow walker and much encumbered with useless baggage of his own, he had one day set out first, the route being quite straight; while the others, knowing that they could easily overtake him, had loitered in their encampment, perhaps an hour after his departure. Aware of his eccentricity, they were not alarmed at not seeing him for the better part of the day ; but as the evening drew in, their fears were excited, and one of the Indians retraced his way, in order to be quite sure that he was not behind among the islands. His search was fruitless, and he very properly returned with the information to the fishery. Mr. McLeod lost not a moment in selecting another Indian to accompany the same person, directing them to use the utmost vigilance, and holding out the promise of a considerable reward to whoever should find him. With such an inducement, it was not likely they would leave any part unexamined; and accordingly, after an absence of three or four days, they returned to the fishery with the assurance that he had not stopped between their last encampment and the islands, from which the traverse is made to the south shore ; on the contrary, they concluded that he had crossed over and made the best of his way to Fort Resolution. For my own part I much doubted this ; but, at all events, it was consolatory to know that he had a compass, and was not destitute of provisions.

. . . .

"On the 3rd June, the whole of the men came in from the fishery and brought with them the melancholy tidings that the Indians had been at Fort Resolution without hearing anything about poor Williamson, who, it was now conjectured, must have got bewildered among the islands away from the track, or met with some accident so as to incapacitate him from making a fire, and thereby indicating his situation.

. . . .

" The faint hope I had entertained of poor Williamson being alive, was extinguished by the intelligence that his body had been found and interred by Mr. McLeod. The unhappy man was discovered

its journey on the 28th June. In April following, as
they were making preparations to ascend the "Thlew-
ee-choh," or Great Fish River, which they had dis-

lying on the ground, with a few sticks near him, not far from his fire.
He had died, it seemed, from famine, aided, perhaps, by the despondency as observable in his conduct for some months previous to his
discharge. The cause of this dejection we were unable to discover;
but so melancholy was he, that in the autumn before the house was
built, and when we were all encamped around it, instead of associating
with his comrades, he built himself a hut with pine branches, in which
he ate his solitary meal; and frequently in the stillness of the night,
when most others were at rest, this extraordinary man would be found
sitting before his dwelling, with his eyes intently fixed on the dying
embers of his fire. He did little duty of any kind, and was treated
with uniform kindness by the whole of the people, who called him
poor David, seeming to regard him as one in deep distress of mind,
whom they were bound to pity. As it often happens to those who go
astray, he was but a short distance from the fishery he had left, and
to which, as was conjectured by his having followed a track made by
some of our men but two days before the ice broke up, he was en-
deavouring to return."

Malley, at one time lost himself among the swamps and rocks,
and was absent for several hours. A party was sent in search of
him, but he chanced to find his own way back to the main body, who
had just accomplished the perilous task of descending a rapid. "Such
incidents (among *voyageurs*)," says Captain Back, generally afford a
name to the spot where they happen; so, to conform to the usage, I
called this 'Malley's Rapid.' "

The Ordnance Corps, whose motto is justly "UBIQUE," has also
been represented in these regions in later years. A party of fifteen
men, selected from a number of volunteers of the Royal Sappers and
Miners, accompanied the expedition under the orders of Sir John
Richardson, in 1848, which searched the shores of the Polar seas
from the Mackenzie to the Coppermine, for traces of the Franklin
expedition. Spirited accounts of the individual exertions and sufferings of this party are given in Sir John Richardson's 'Journal of
a Boat Voyage through Rupert's Land and the Arctic,' and are
more especially brought to notice in Mr. Connolly's excellent 'History of the Royal Sappers and Miners.'

covered in August, intelligence arrived of the safety of Captain Ross and his crew. Back thus describes the manner in which he received the intelligence :— " We were talking for about the hundredth time of those kind persons who had come so far to see us away, when we were interrupted by a sharp and loud knock at the door. The permission to come in was unnecessary, for the person followed the announcement before the words could be uttered, and with the same dispatch thrust into my hands a packet, which a glance sufficed to tell me was from England. ' He is returned, Sir ! ' said the messenger, as we looked at him with surprise. ' What ! Augustus ? thank God ! ' I replied quickly. ' Captain Ross, Sir; Captain Ross is returned.' ' Eh ! are you quite sure ? is there no error ? where is the account from ? ' The man paused, looked at me, and pointing with his finger said, ' You have it in your hand, Sir. ' It was so ; but the packet had been forgotten in the excitement and hurry of my feelings. Two open extracts from the *Times* and the *Morning Herald* confirmed the tidings ; and my official letter, with others from the long-lost adventurers themselves, removed all possible doubt. In the fulness of our hearts we assembled together, and humbly offered up our thanks to that merciful Providence, who, in the beautiful language of scripture, hath said, ' Mine own will I bring again, as I did sometime from the deep of the sea.* The thought of so wonderful a preserva-

* Psalm 68.

tion overpowered for a time the common occurrences of life. We had just sat down to breakfast; but our appetite was gone, and the day was passed in a feverish state of excitement. Seldom, indeed, did my friend Mr. King or I indulge in a libation, but on this joyful occasion economy was forgotten; a treat was given to the men, and for ourselves the social sympathies were quickened by a generous bowl of punch."

As the preparations were completed, however, Back did not return, but pushed on his discoveries; navigated the whole of the Fish River (since called after him, " Back's Fish River ") and discovered Montreal Island, Adelaide Peninsula, &c. They suffered greatly from cold and hunger during part of this journey; Back writing in January, 1834, says: " A few days exhausted our small stock of meat, and I reluctantly opened another bag of pemmican, our store of which was now reduced to less than one half of the quantity originally put aside for sea service. Mr. King and I contented ourselves with half-a-pound each a day; but the labouring men whom we retained with us could not do with less than a pound and three-quarters. Even this was but scanty rations; nevertheless, the fine fellows (principally artillerymen), far from being moody or sullen, were always cheerful and in good spirits." And on the 4th February following:—" Such was the abstraction of heat, that, with eight large logs of wood in the fire-place of a small room, I could not get the thermometer higher

than 13° plus. Ink and paint froze. The sextant
cases, and boxes of seasoned wood, principally fir, all
split. Nor was the sensation particularly agreeable
to our persons; the skin of the hands especially
became dry, cracked, and opened into unsightly and
smarting gashes, which we were obliged to anoint
with grease. On one occasion, after washing my
face within three feet of the fire, my hair was actually
clotted with ice before I had time to dry it. From
these facts some idea may perhaps be formed of the
excessive cold."

They all, however, with one exception, returned
safe to Fort Reliance (a post of the Hudson's Bay
Company), from whence Captain Back started for
Canada, and from thence proceeded home, arriving
in Liverpool on the 8th September, 1835. Dr. King,
with the remainder of the party, reached England in
October.

. . . .

Captain Ross and his crew had been frozen in in
the Gulf of Boothia, from October, 1829, until
August, 1833, subsisting, during the two latter
winters, on the provisions which Parry left at Fury
Beach.

During this period many discoveries were made.
Felix Harbour, in the Gulf of Boothia (which is a
continuation of Regent's Inlet), where they passed
their first winter, was 300 miles south of Parry's
farthest, and much of the coast, in all directions from

this point, was explored by land parties. In May, 1830, Commander James Ross, with Mr. Blanky, and two Esquimaux guides, crossed the Isthmus of Boothia and discovered Matty Island, and King William's Land, which was supposed to be the mainland of America. From the northermost point of King William's Land, which they named Cape Felix, they proceeded in a south-westerly direction, a distance of twenty miles, but anxious as they were to proceed, they were without the means of subsistence for doing so. As this spot in after years became a place of interest, I will give Commander Ross' account of his visit to it :—" We now therefore unfurled our flag for the usual ceremony, and took possession of what we saw as far as the distant point, while that on which we stood was named Victory Point, being the *ne plus ultra* of our labour, as it afterwards proved, while it will remain a standing record of the exertions of that ship's crew. The point to the south-west was named Cape Franklin, and if that be a name which has now been conferred on more places than one, these honours—not in fact very solid when so widely shared—are, beyond all thought, less than the merits which that officer deserves.*

On Victory Point we erected a cairn of stones six feet high, and we enclosed in it a canister containing a brief account of the proceedings of the expedition

* It was almost within sight of this spot the gallant Franklin breathed his last.

since its departure from England. Such has been the custom, and to that it was our business to conform; though I must say that we did not entertain the most remote hope that our little history would ever meet an European's eye, even had it escaped the accident of falling into the hands of the Esquimaux."

On the 1st June, 1831, Captain Ross discovered the position of the "*Magnetic Pole*," which, for centuries, had been an object of ungratified curiosity to the civilized world. In Lat. 70° 5′ 17″ N., and Long. 96° 46′ 45′ W., Ross placed a British flag, and took possession of the Magnetic Pole and its adjoining territory, in the name of Great Britain and King William the Fourth. But as " Nature had here erected no monument to denote the spot which she had chosen as the centre of one of her great and dark powers," they erected a cairn of some magnitude, and placed in it a record of the fact.* On the 29th May, 1832, the *Victory* was abandoned, being the first vessel Sir John Ross had ever been obliged to leave, after having served in thirty-six, during a period of forty-two years. The crew proceeded to Fury Beach, where they built a hut, which they named " Somerset House; " here they remained until July, 1833, when they took their departure in boats, being fortunate

* This is not the precise position of the Magnetic Pole, for the dip was 89° 59′, which is one minute of the vertical position ; but as, with the instruments they had, they could approach no nearer to 90°, Capt. Ross felt himself justified in marking this spot as the " throne of magnetism."

enough (on the 26th August) to fall in with the
Isabella, whaler, which was the first ship Ross sailed
in to the Arctic regions. Captain Ross was told
circumstantially of his own death, &c., two years
previously, and he had some difficulty in convincing
them that it was really he and his party who now
stood before them. So great was the joy with which
they were received, that the *Isabella* manned her
yards, and her former commander and his gallant
band of adventurers were saluted with three hearty
cheers. The scene on board can scarcely be described; each of the crew vied with the other in
assisting and comforting the party, and it cannot
better be told than in Ross' own words :—

" The ludicrous soon took place of all other feelings ;
in such a crowd, and such confusion, all serious
thought was impossible, while the new buoyancy of
our spirits made us abundantly willing to be amused
by the scene which now opened. Every man was
hungry, and was to be fed; all were ragged, and were
to be clothed; there was not one to whom washing
was not indispensable, nor one whom his beard did
not deprive of all human semblance. All, everything
too, was to be done at once : it was washing, dressing,
shaving, eating, all intermingled ; it was all the
materials of each jumbled together, while in the midst
of all there were interminable questions to be asked
and answered on both sides ; the adventures of the
Victory, our own escapes, the politics of England, and
the news which was now four years old.

" But all subsided into peace at last. The sick were accommodated, the seamen disposed of, and all was done for us which care and kindness could perform.

" Night at length brought quiet and serious thoughts,—and I trust there was not a man among us who did not then express, where it was due, his gratitude for that interposition which had raised us all from a despair which none could now forget, and had brought us from the very borders of a most distant grave, to life, and friends, and civilization. Long accustomed, however, to a cold bed on the hard snow or the bare rock, few could sleep amid the com-‧fort of our new accommodations. I was myself compelled to leave the bed which had been kindly assigned me, and take my abode in a chair for the night; nor did it fare much better with the rest. It was for time to reconcile us to this sudden and violent change, to break through what had become habit, and to inure us once more to the usages of our former days."

They arrived at home on the 18th September. The bold explorers were looked upon as men risen from the dead, and met and escorted by crowds of sympathisers. The crew received double pay from the government for the time they had been absent; Captain John Ross received the honour of knighthood and had a gratuity of £5,000 granted him; while a baronetcy was conferred on Mr. Felix Booth.*

* Sir Felix Booth died at Brighton in 1850, aged 95 years.

This was the last attempt to discover the North-
West Passage until the departure of the *Erebus* and
Terror.

Captain Back made a voyage in the *Terror* in 1836,
with the intention of reaching Wager River, via
Hudson's Strait: he only reached the Frozen Strait,
however, where the ship was so dreadfully shattered
by the ice that it was with difficulty he was able to
return.

In 1837-8 Messrs. Thomas Simpson and Peter
Warren Dease (officers of the Hudson's Bay Comp.),
traced all the northern coast of America from Franklin's Farthest, at the mouth of the Coppermine, to
Back's Farthest, at Point Ogle, and discovered Victoria Land and the southern shore of King William's
Land, where, on the 25th August, 1839, they erected
a cairn on a spot named Cape Herschel.

PART II.

———

" Whither am *I going ?*
Into eternity! that boundless sea,
Fast as the streams of time can glide away.
Oh! thou eternity! thou awful sound,
Thou searchless ocean, and thou deep profound,
'Midst thine infinitudes my thoughts are drown'd
Compared with thee, how scanty *Time* appears;
How mere a nothing is our three-score years!
Yet for this short duration I've no lease;
'Tenant at will,' and 'quit' when God shall please;
Howe'er protracted, life is but 'a span,'
Short the existence of the oldest man.—TARRANT."

*A Brief Sketch of Franklin's History—His Departure
in 1845—Prolonged Absence and Various Searching
Expeditions—Discovery of the North-West Passage
Dr. Rae—Relics and Information obtained from the
Esquimaux—The Resolute.*

In 1845, the Lords Commissioners of the Admiralty, at the instigation of Sir John Barrow, determined on sending out *one more* expedition, on a larger scale than any previous ones, to solve the problem of the North-West Passage. Accordingly the command was given to Sir John Franklin, who commissioned the *Erebus* and *Terror*, two vessels which had but lately returned from a successful voyage in the South

Polar Seas. The entire crews, consisting of 137 men, were volunteers, and,—though it was known that none but unexceptionable characters would be accepted,—the applications for appointments were so numerous, that, had the Lords of the Admiralty chosen, they could have manned the ships with petty officers. The brave Sir John himself, afraid they would not allow him to go if they knew he was 60 years old, took advantage of the three weeks he was short of that age to enter himself as 59. Lord Haddington, who was the First Lord of the Admiralty, sent for Sir Edward Parry, and said : " I see by looking at the Navy List that Franklin is 60 years old : do you think we ought to let him go ? " The answer of that great man was : " He is a fitter man than any I know ; and if you don't let him go he will die of disappointment."

Sir John Franklin was born at Spilsby, in Lincolnshire, in 1786. He entered the Navy in 1800, and served as a midshipman in the action off Copenhagen, in the following year. He next sailed on a voyage of discovery to New Holland, during which he suffered shipwreck—on a coral reef near Cato Bank—August 17th, 1803. Here he spent nearly two months, with his fellow sufferers, on a narrow sand-bank, only a few feet above the sea level, whilst Capt. Flinders (the commander of the wrecked vessel) proceeded to Port Jackson for relief. They were taken up by the *Porpoise*, Capt. Fowler, and conveyed to Canton, where they embarked in the *Earl Camden*, commanded by Sir Nathaniel Dance, for England. This vessel was attacked by the French in the Straits of Malacca, but Sir Nathaniel, with the brave seamen under his command, gallantly defeated his antagonist. The next great affair we find Franklin engaged in, was the ever memorable Battle of Trafalgar, in 1805, where he served on board the *Bellerophon*. He afterwards served in the Channel Fleet, and at the blockade of Flushing; and in 1808, being then lieutenant, escorted the Royal Family of Portugal from Lisbon to Brazil. He was engaged in very arduous services during the American War of 1814, and was wounded in a boat engagement before New Orleans. In 1818 he commanded the *Trent* on the perilous voyage of discovery in the neighbourhood of Spitzbergen, which has before been mentioned. In April, 1819, he was invested with the command of an expedition to proceed overland from Hudson's Bay to the Coppermine River, where he endured sufferings unparalleled in history. He effected a journey of 5,550 miles, undergoing the greatest possible hardships and privations, during which he traced the whole of the Coppermine River, and some miles of the shores of the Polar Sea. To give an idea of what he and his party* suffered

* Franklin's party in this expedition consisted of Dr. Richardson, Mr. Hood, and Mr. (now Sir George) Back, midshipmen; a seaman named Hepburn, 16 Canadians, Mr. F. Wentzell, and 3 Indians. Mr. Hood and two of the Canadians were murdered by an Iroquois named "Michel," who, in turn, was shot by Dr. Richardson. Three other Canadians also perished—two from want, the other was frozen to death.

during this expedition, a few extracts from his narrative are here introduced :—

"Having walked twelve miles and a half, we encamped at 7 P.M., and distributed our last piece of pemmican and a little arrowroot for supper, which afforded but a scanty meal. As we had nothing to eat, and were destitute of the means of making a fire, we remained in our beds all the day; but the covering of our blankets was insufficient to prevent us from feeling the severity of the frost, and suffering inconvenience from the drifting of the snow into our tents. There was no abatement of the storm next day; our tents were completely frozen, and the snow had drifted around them to a depth of three feet, and even in the inside there was a covering of several inches on our blankets.

"Our suffering from cold, in a comfortless canvass tent in such weather, with the temperature at 20°, and without fire, will easily be imagined; it was, however, less than that which we felt from hunger."

"Occasionally they picked up pieces of skin, and a few bones of deer which had been devoured by the wolves in the previous spring. The bones were rendered friable by burning, and now and then their old shoes were added to the repast.—SIMMONDS."

"After halting an hour, during which we refreshed ourselves with eating our old shoes and a few scraps of leather, &c.—FRANKLIN."

Dr. Richardson was for a time separated from Franklin, and he thus describes their re-union:—

"Upon entering the desolate dwelling, we had the satisfaction of embracing Captain Franklin, but no words can convey an idea of the filth and wretchedness that met our eyes on looking around. Our own misery had stolen upon us by degrees, and we were accustomed to the contemplation of each other's emaciated figures; but the ghastly countenances, dilated eye-balls, and sepulchral voices of Captain Franklin and those with him were more than we could at first bear."

. . . .

"Hepburn having shot a partridge, which was brought to the house, the doctor tore out the feathers, and having held it to the fire a few minutes, divided it into six portions. I and my three companions ravenously devoured our shares, as it was the first morsel of flesh any of us had tasted for thirty-one days.—FRANKLIN."

On the 16th of February, 1825, this energetic officer again left England on another expedition to the Frozen Regions, having for its object a co-operation with Captains F. W. Beechey and W. E. Parry, in ascertaining from opposite quarters the existence of a north-west passage. The result of this mission will be found in detail in Captain Franklin's "Narrative of a Second Expedition to the Shores of the Polar Sea in 1825-7."

On his return to England, where he arrived on the 26th of ·September, 1827, Franklin was presented by the Geographical Society of Paris with a gold medal valued at 1,200 francs, for having made the most important acquisitions to geographical knowledge during the preceding year, and on the 29th of April, 1829, he received the honour of knighthood, besides being awarded in July following the Oxford degree of a D.C.L.

From 1830 to 1834 he was in active service in command of H.M.S. *Rainbow* on the Mediterranean station, and for his exertions during that period as connected with the troubles in Greece, was presented with the order of the Redeemer, of Greece. Sir John was created a K.C.H. on the 25th of January, 1836, and was for some time Governor of Van Dieman's Land.

He married, on the 16th of August, 1823, Eleanor Anne,* youngest daughter of W. Porden, Esq.,

---

* Mrs. Eleanor Anne Franklin, better know by her maiden name, Miss Porden, was a poetess of no mean pretensions. Her acquaintance with Captain Franklin originated at the commencement of that Arctic Expedition (1818), in which, as is proved by a poem of hers published at the time, her sympaties were warmly engaged. Her first publication was a poem dedicated to the Countess Spencer, entitled " THE VEILS, OR THE TRIALS OF CONSTANCY," which appeared in 1815; her greatest work, however, was en epic poem on the third crusade, entitled " CŒUR DE LION," which was dedicated (by permission) to the King (1822). She was married to Capt. Franklin on the 23rd August, 1823, and, in the following June, gave birth to a daughter, now the wife of the Rev. Philip Gell, of Tasmania. She died on the 22nd February, 1825, six days after Franklin took his departure for North America.

architect, of Berners Street, London ; and secondly, on the 5th of November, 1828, Jane, second daughter of John Griffin, Esq., of Bedford Place.

Sir John Franklin was a man beloved by all classes, at all times.

Sir Edward Parry, in a speech made at a dinner given to Lieut. Creswell, at Lynn, in 1853, said :—

"In the whole course of my experience I have never known a man like Franklin. I do not say it because he is dead—upon the principle *de mortuis nil nisi bonum;* but I never knew a man in whom different qualities were so remarkably combined. In my dear friend Franklin, with all the tenderness of heart of a simple child, there was all the greatness and magnanimity of a hero."

Captain Back relates the following anecdote :—

" It was the custom of Sir John Franklin never to kill a fly ; and, though teased by them beyond expression, especially when engaged in taking observations, he would quietly desist from his work, and patiently blow the half-gorged intruders from his hands—'The world was wide enough for both.'"

Captain Fitzjames, writing from the Orkneys, in June, 1845, says :—

" Sir John Franklin is delightful, active, energetic, and evidently even now persevering. What he has been we all know. I think it will turn out that he is nowise altered. He is full of conversation and interesting anecdotes of his former voyages. I would not lose him for the command of the expedition, for I have a real regard—I may say, affection—for him, and I believe this is felt by all of us."

And a letter from Lieutenant Fairholme contains the following :—

" On board, we are as comfortable as it is possible to be. I need hardly tell you how much we are all delighted with our captain. He has, I am sure, won not only the respect but the love of every person on board, by his amiable manner and kindness to all ; and his influence is always employed for some good purpose, both among the officers and men. He has been most successful in his selection of officers, and a more agreeable set could hardly be found."

That he was not only beloved by officers, is proved by the fact that, when in command in the Mediterranean (1834), his ship (the *Rainbow*), was called by all the sailors of the fleet, the " *Celestial Rainbow*," and " *Franklin's Paradise*."

· " Captain Crozier was in all Parry's expeditions, having been midshipman in the *Fury* in 1821, and in the *Hecla* in 1824 ; he went out as a lieutenant in the *Hecla* with Parry on his boat expedition to the Pole in 1827 ; volunteered in 1836 to go out in search of the missing whalers and their crews to Davis Straits ; was made a captain in 1841 ; and was second in command of the Antarctic expedition under Sir James Ross, and on his return was appointed to the *Terror* as second in command under Franklin."

Captain Fitzjames, an officer greatly beloved in the service, who distinguished himself on the Euphrates expedition and in Syria, and had been severely wounded in China, was appointed as second to Sir John Franklin, and to conduct the magnetic observations.

With such men as leaders, it is not to be wondered at if the choicest spirits in the service sought to be followers, and if among the crews of the *Erebus* and *Terror* mustering a band of 137 persons, were found to be officers as good, and seamen as stout and brave, as ever trod the deck of a man-of-war.

On Monday, 19th of May, 1845, the *Erebus* and *Terror* sailed from Greenhithe on this gallant enterprize. Their last anchorage in sight of Britain was at the Long Hope, Orkneys, from whence they departed on the 8th June, full of hope.

> " A desert waste of waters lies before—
> Behind, the anxious hospitable shore,
> Which like a parent bird sees ye depart,
> Bold winged messengers of daring Art!
> We know that sunshine always 'round your path
> Cannot attend ; that rain and tempest's wrath
> Will be your portion ; but our pray'r shall be
> You live their fury out right gallantly,
> And after years you have perchance to roam
> That science crown'd you safely seek your home!—W."*

A month later they were at the Whale Fish Islands, loading from the *Baretto* transport, which parted from them on the 13th July. A fortnight after, they were

* *Illustrated London News*, May, 1845.

seen by Capt. Dannet, of the *Prince of Wales*, whaler, who was visited by seven of the officers. These reported that "all were well, in excellent spirits, and confident of success." That same evening (July 26th), the ice opened out, and the *Erebus* and *Terror* made direct for Lancaster Sound. The masts of the vessels soon lessened in the horizon, and were hidden from the sight of the whalers, never again to be seen by the civilized world.

Towards the end of 1847, nothing having been heard of Sir John Franklin's expedition, various proposals were made by different persons as to the mode, time, and place of sending relief to them. Among these,—alas ! now seen too late—was one from Dr. King, the companion of Back in 1833, who proposed, and also volunteered, to go by way of the Great Fish River to the Arctic Seas. This was dated February, 1848, and we know now that had an expedition gone by that route—at that time—they would, in all probability, have saved 105 of those gallant men.

But many other propositions were submitted, and by far more experienced Arctic travellers than Dr. King, and it is but natural to suppose they would receive the earliest attention.

In the early part of 1848, however, three expeditions were sent in quest, and for the aid of Sir John and his crews. The first, the *Plover*, under the command of Captain Moore, sailed in January, for Behring's Strait; the second, under Sir John Richard-

son, searched the northern coast of America, from the
Mackenzie to the Coppermine; and the third, the
Enterprise and *Investigator*, Sir James Ross, started
in June for Lancaster Sound, which was reached by
the 26th August. This expedition carefully searched
the western coast of North Somerset and Prince of
Wales' Land, and wintering at Port Leopold, returned
in 1849, unsuccessful. Sir John Richardson also
returned in 1849, having gained no tidings of Sir
John Franklin; and the *Plover*, which did not reach
its destination until after the arrival of the others in
England, returned in 1852.

In 1850, a determined and combined attempt was
made to discover and relieve the missing navigators,
and, in the same year, the following rewards were
offered by Government:—

"To any party or person who, in the judgment of
the Board of Admiralty, shall discover and effectually
relieve the crews of H. M. Ships *Erebus* and *Terror*,
the sum of £20,000.

"To any party or parties, &c., who shall discover
and effectually relieve any portion of the crews, or
shall convey such intelligence as shall lead to the
relief of any of the crew, the sum of £10,000.

"To any party or parties who shall, by his or their
efforts, first succeed in ascertaining their fate,
£10,000."

In 1848, 100 guineas had been offered to any
whaler who might bring information of the missing

F

expedition; and at the same time Lady Franklin offered rewards of £2,000, and £3,000 to any crew bringing them to England.

The *Enterprise*, Captain Collinson, and the *Investigator*, Captain M'Clure, started in January to pursue the search, by way of Behring's Strait; and in May following, the *Resolute*, Captain Austin, the *Assistance*, Captain Ommaney, the *Intrepid*, Lieut. Cator, the *Pioneer*, Lieutenant Osborn, the *Lady Franklin*, Captain Penny,* and the *Sophia*, Captain Stewart,* left the Thames *en route* to Lancaster Sound.

In addition to these Government expeditions, Lady Franklin despatched the *Prince Albert*, Captain Forsyth; Sir John Ross, aided by the Hudson's Bay Company, went in his own yatcht, the *Felix*; and our Transatlantic brethren sent two ships, which were presented for the purpose by Mr. Grinnel, of New York—the *Advance*, Lieutenant De Haven, and *Rescue*, Lieutenant Griffin,—making a total of twelve vessels, all engaged in the one great object: that of seeking and assisting the lost loved ones. Much geographical knowledge was acquired by these searching expeditions, indeed Capt. Stewart, of the *Sophia*, to his great astonishment, found himself on the verge of the open Polar Sea, the existence of which had long been a theoretical question, and where it was believed by many Sir John Franklin had penetrated.

* Officers of the Merchant Service.

Having no boats, however, Captain Stewart could not sail upon this newly discovered sea.

Notwithstanding the hundreds of miles travelled by sea and land, the daring, energy, and endurance displayed by our countrymen in these expeditions, all the information they could obtain of the lost ones was that they had wintered at Beechey Island in 1845-6; three graves, with head-boards,* and various articles strewed about, being found there by Captain Penny.

On the shore of North Devon, the east side of Wellington Channel, Captain Penny also picked up a piece of paper, having on it (in the writing of Capt. Fitzjames) the following words :—" *Call me at four o'clock to-morrow.*"

From Cape Spenser, where this paper was picked up, the Americans traced the trail of a sledge beyond Cape Innis, where it suddenly ceased. Here was found a bottle and a piece of the *Times* newspaper.

During the winter of 1850-1 (which was unusually severe) the commanders of the different vessels outvied each other in providing recreation and amusements for the men under their command. The crew of one ship frequently invited that of another to a ball, a concert, or perhaps an *evening* party ; and the guests, so as not to miss their way returning, generally placed finger-posts at intervals between their own vessel and that of their entertainers.

* See Appendix No. 5.

"In going from one ship to another during the night, there was a danger of being attacked by bears, so that, instead of dining yourself, you ran the risk of serving as a dinner for one of these disagreeable animals."* On one occasion a masquerade ball was given on board the *Assistance,* and a number of each ship's crew were invited: they kept it up with a good grace, and their enjoyment was quite as genuine (if not more so), as that of guests at the finest ball in England. They separated early, or rather late, in the morning, after a deal of parley and ordering on the part of the officers: one sailor so enjoyed himself that he continued to sing, in a most lusty manner, "He wouldn't go home till morning till daylight did appear," an assertion which, if persevered in, would have necessitated his staying some six weeks, if not for a longer period. On board the *Assistance* they had first-rate theatrical performances; a pantomime, entitled *Zero,* written on the subject of their situation, was produced on boxing day. They also got up a newspaper entitled the "*Illustrated Arctic News,*" the illustrations of which consisted of pencil sketches and water-colour drawings, executed by themselves. The paper was circulated from ship to ship.

All the vessels which entered the Arctic seas by Baffin's Bay returned home in 1851, none of them having fell in with those which went by Behring's Strait.

* Arctic Miscellanies.

In 1851, Lady Franklin again sent out the *Prince Albert*, in charge of Captain Kennedy, and Lieut. Bellot, an officer of the French Navy. It returned in 1852, however, after a fruitless search in Regent's Inlet. A strait connecting this inlet and the waters on the west side of Boothia, was discovered by Capt. Kennedy, who named it after his companion, "Bellot Strait."

In 1852, Captain Inglefield searched the head of Baffin's Bay, and examined its large sounds and straits. He penetrated into Whale Sound for a number of miles, but was driven back by continued heavy gales.

In the same year another expedition, under the command of Sir Edward Belcher, consisting of the *Assistance* (Belcher), the *Pioneer*, (Osborn), the *Resolute* (Kellett), the *Intrepid*, (McClintock), and the *North Star* (Mr. Pullen), was sent, not only to continue the search for Sir John Franklin, but also to try and obtain some tidings of the *Investigator* and *Enterprise*, which left England in January, 1850, and were seen for the last time in August of the same year.

This fleet reached Melville Sound, from whence sledge parties were dispatched in every possible direction. In the summer of 1853, Captain Kellett, of the *Resolute* (who was the officer commanding the *Herald*, when that vessel parted with the *Investigator* at the Sandwich Islands in 1850), found in Winter

Harbour, Melville Island, a dispatch from Captain M'Clure, which contained the following information :

" On the 7th September, 1850, he discovered land, which he named ' Baring Island,' the north of which is the ' Bank's Land ' of Parry.

" On the 9th, he discovered land, which he named ' Prince Albert's Land,' and which, with ' Victoria ' and ' Wollaston ' lands, form one large island.

" On the 13th October, he discovered a number of small islands which he named the ' Princess Royal Isles,' and on the 26th entered Barrow Strait, in Lat. 73° 30′ N., Long. 114° 14′ W., by a strait which he called ' Prince of Wales Strait,' thereby establishing the existence of a ' NORTH-WEST PASSAGE.'

" During this winter (1850-1), he was ' frozen in ' in the new Prince of Wales Strait, and ever since the 24th September, 1851, he had been imprisoned in a small harbour north of Baring Island ; but in April, 1852, he had crossed the ice with a sledge party and deposited the dispatch."

Captain Kellett immediately sent Lieutenant Pim and a party to their relief, who discovered them (for the most part) very ill and forlorn looking, they, in addition to their imprisonment, having been on reduced rations for two years.

Captain Kellett's account of the discovery of the *Investigator* by Pim, is thus given :—

" M'Clure and his First Lieutenant were walking on the floe, and seeing a person coming very fast

towards them, they supposed he was chased by a bear
or had seen a bear, and walked towards him: on getting
onwards a hundred yards, they could see from his proportions that he was not one of them. Pim began to
screech and throw up his hands (his face as black as
my hat); this brought the captain and lieutenant to a
stand, as they could not hear sufficienly to make out
his language.

"At length Pim reached the party, quite beside
himself, and stammered out, on M'Clure asking him,
'Who are you, and where are you come from?'—
'Lieutenant Pim, *Herald*, Captain Kellett.' This
was more inexplicable to M'Clure, as I was the last
person he shook hands with in Behring's Straits. He
at length found that this solitary stranger was a true
Englishman—an angel of light; he says—' He soon
was seen from the ship—they had only one hatchway
open, and the crew were fairly jammed there, in their
endeavour to get up. The sick jumped out of their
hammocks, and the crew forgot their despondency;
in fact, all was changed on board the *Investigator*."

M'Clure named the spot where his ship was imprisoned, "Mercy Bay."

This news, and also the sick of the *Investigator*,
were brought home by Captain Inglefield, in the
Phœnix. He also brought the melancholy intelligence of the death of Lieutenant Bellot, of the French
Navy, who had volunteered and served in two expeditions in search of Sir John Franklin. It appears

that this noble seaman was blown away from the
shore, in company with two seamen, upon a floe of
ice. He had mounted to the top of a hummock in
order to reconnoitre the position, and to see what
could be done for the safety of his two companions.
At this moment he was taken by the wind, thrown
into a crack in the ice, and unfortunately drowned.
The two men were saved, after driving about for thirty
hours, without food or hope. The records of Arctic
heroism can show no brighter name than that of
Bellot. He was endeared to all his English shipmates
by every social quality, as well as by his unflinching
valour and daring. Our countrymen have done justice
to his virtues by raising a subscription for his family,
and erecting three monuments to his memory, viz.:
one on Beechey Island,* one in Greenwich Hospital,†
and a tablet in one of the churches of Paris.

"The indifference with which the announced discovery of the North-West Passage was generally
received, both in England and in America, was somewhat surprising. The existence of such a passage had

* See Appendix No. 5.

† An obelisk of Aberdeen granite, on which the following inscription appears:—

"To the intrepid young
BELLOT,
Who, in the endeavour to rescue
FRANKLIN,
Shared the fate and the glory of that
Illustrious Navigator.
From his British admirers.
1853."

been for three centuries reckoned among the most difficult and doubtful of geographical problems. Great prizes have been offered by public bodies and by private individuals for its practical solution; and expedition after expedition has been fitted out at vast expense to carry on the investigation. For this object hardships have been endured and dangers run in the Arctic seas such as can be found in no other maritime record. And yet, after all, when the result of this long research has been attained, and sober certainty takes the place of imaginative doubt, the fact does not even excite the interest of a nine days' wonder. It mixes in with the current of ordinary events, and quickly passes from attention. This is owing mainly to two reasons—the impression of the utter uselessness of the discovery for all practical purposes, and the universal feeling of regret that the lives of so many gallant men should have been sacrificed for such an end. The fact that Captain M'Clure, of the *Investigator*, of whom, for the last three years, more has been expected in the work of discovering traces of Sir John Franklin, than of any other individual, has not been able to obtain the least clue to the object of his search, has done much in destroying the interest in what he actually did accomplish. For years he was where no other ship had ever been before him. He had discovered new land, defined a long extent of coast line that was before uncertain, held intercourse with a new people, and verified the

G

existence of a North-West Passage, and yet effected nothing of the business on which the ship was specially despatched. The discovery of Sir John Franklin would have been worth the discovery of a North-West Passage a thousand times over.— (SIMMONDS).

The *Enterprize*, Captain Collinson, which left England with M'Clure in the *Investigator*, wintered in 1850-1 at Hong-Kong, and in the following summer entered the ice. She found traces of the *Investigator's* passage in many places, and went within ninety miles of her winter harbour, but not being able to proceed farther on account of the ice, sailed up to Wollaston Strait, and there fell in with traces of Dr. Rae's searches. In 1851-2 their winter-quarters were in Prince of Wales' Strait; in 1852-3 they were frozen in in Cambridge Bay, Wollaston Land; and the winter of 1853-4 was passed in Camden Bay. On the 15th July, 1854, they were extricated from the ice, and commenced their return passage, arriving in England on the 21st August, 1855. While in Cambridge Bay, Captain Collinson picked up a portion of a companion door, with the Queen's arms stamped upon it. Subsequent discoveries have confirmed the original idea that this relic belonged to the missing vessels, as the strait in which they were abandoned is a continuation of Dease Strait, one of the inlets of which is Cambridge Bay. Captain M'Clure's ship, the *Investigator*, is still in the ice in Mercy Bay, he and his crew having left the Arctic regions, through Baffin's Bay, in the *Phœnix*, in 1854.

In May, 1854, Sir Edward Belcher ordered the whole of the ships under his command—the *Assistance*, the *Resolute*, the *Pioneer*, and the *Intrepid*—to be abandoned. They were frozen up in Melville Sound, and the crews had to travel on foot from thence to Beechey Island, where they were taken up and conveyed home, by the *North Star*, *Phœnix*, and *Talbot*, store-ships. On his return, which was at the commencement of the Russian campaign, he was ordered to publish his narrative under the title of "THE LAST OF THE ARCTIC VOYAGES,"—the *Erebus* and *Terror* were struck off the Navy List, and the families of the missing seamen paid up to the 31st March, 1854.

A few months after the return of Sir Edward Belcher, just as the friends of the lost ones were reconciling themselves to the unhappy issue of all the searching expeditions, the country was startled by the arrival of Dr. Rae, of the Hudson's Bay Company, with a number of relics of the ill-fated mariners, which he had obtained from the Esquimaux at Pelly Bay.

The following is Dr. Rae's Report to the Secretary of the Admiralty: "*Repulse Bay, July* 29.

"SIR,—I have the honour to mention, for the information of my Lords Commissioners of the Admiralty, that during my journey over the ice and snow this spring, with the view of completing the survey of the west shore of Boothia, I met with Esquimaux in

Pelly Bay, from one of whom I learned that a party
of 'white men' (Kablounans), had perished from want
of food some distance to the westward, and not far
beyond a large river, containing many falls and rapids.
Subsequently, further particulars were received, and
a number of articles purchased, which place the
fate of a portion, if not of all, of the then survivors of
Sir John Franklin's long-lost party beyond a doubt—
a fate terrible as the imagination can conceive.

"The substance of the information obtained at
various times and from various sources was as follows:

"In the spring, four winters past (spring 1850), a
party of 'white men,' amounting to about forty, were
seen travelling southward over the ice and dragging
a boat with them, by some Esquimaux, who were
killing seals near the north shore of King William's
Land, which is a large island. None of the party
could speak the Esquimaux language intelligibly, but
by signs the natives were made to understand that
their ship, or ships, had been crushed by ice, and that
they were now going to where they expected to find
deer to shoot. From the appearance of the men, all
of whom, except one officer, looked thin, they were
then supposed to be getting short of provisions, and
purchased a small seal from the natives. At a later
date the same season, but previous to the breaking up
of the ice, the bodies of some thirty persons were
discovered on the continent, and five on an island near
it, about a long day's journey to the north-west of a

large stream, which can be no other than Back's
Great Fish River, (named by the Esquimaux Doot-
ko-hi-calik) as its description, and that of the low
shore in the neighbourhood of Point Ogle and Montreal Island agree exactly with that of Sir George
Back. Some of the bodies had been buried (probably
those of the first victims of famine), some were in a
tent or tents, others under the boat which had been
turned over to form a shelter, and several lay scattered about in different directions. Of those found
on the island one was supposed to have been an officer,
as he had a telescope strapped over his shoulders, and
his double-barrelled gun lay underneath him.

" From the mutilated state of many of the corpses,
and the contents of the kettles, it is evident that our
wretched countrymen had been driven to the last
resource—cannibalism—as a means of prolonging
existence.

" There appeared to have been an abundant stock
of ammunition, as the powder was emptied in a heap
on the ground by the natives out of the kegs or cases
containing it; and a quantity of ball and shot was
found below high-water mark, having probably been
left on the ice close to the beach. There must have
been a number of watches, compasses, telescopes, guns
(several double-barrelled), &c., all of which appear to
have been broken up, as I saw pieces of those different
articles with the Esquimaux, together with some
silver spoons and forks. I purchased as many as I

could get. A list of the most important of these I enclose, with a rough sketch of the crests and initials of the forks and spoons. The articles themselves shall be handed over to the Secretary of the Hudson's Bay Company on my arrival in London.

"None of the Esquimaux with whom I conversed had seen the "whites," nor had they ever been at the place where the bodies were found, but had their information from those who had been there, and who had seen the party when travelling.

" I offer no apology for taking the liberty of addressing you, as I do so from a belief that their Lordships would be desirous of being put in possession, at as early a date as possible, of any tidings, however meagre and unexpectedly obtained, regarding this painfully interesting subject.

" I may add that, by means of our guns and nets, we obtained an ample supply of provisions last autumn, and my small party passed the winter in snow houses in comparative comfort, the skins of the deer shot affording abundant warm clothing and bedding. My spring journey was a failure, in consequence of an accumulation of obstacles, several of which my former experience in Arctic travelling had not taught me to expect.

"I have, &c.,

"JOHN RAE, C.F.,

" Commanding Hudson's Bay Comp's.

" Arctic Expedition."

" List of articles purchased from the Esquimaux, said to have been obtained at the place where the bodies of the persons reported to have died of famine were found, viz. :—

1 silver table fork* .. Crest No. 1	1 silv.table fork,intls. H.D.S.G. 1
3 „ „ „ .. „ „ 2	1 „ „ „ „ A. McD. 2
1 „ „ spoon .. „ „ 3	1 „ „ „ „ G. A. M. 3
1 „ „ „ .. „ „ 4	1 „ „ „ „ I. T.
Motto : " Spero Meliora."	1 „ dessert spoon,, J. S. P. 4
1 „ „ fork .. „ „ 4	1 round silver plate, engraved,
Motto : " Spero Meliora."	" Sir John Franklin, K.C.B."
1 „ dessert fork .. „ „ 5	1 star or order, with motto, " Nec
1 „ table spoon .. „ „ 5	aspera terrent," on one side, and
1 „ tea „ .. „ „ 5	on the reverse 'G.R. MDCCCXV.'5

" Also a number of other articles with no marks by which they could be recognised; but which will be handed over, with those above-named, to the Secretary of the Hon. Hudson's Bay Company.

" JOHN RAE, C.F.

" *Repulse Bay, July,* 1854."

Immediately upon the receipt of this news, the Hudson's Bay Company dispatched a boat party up the Great Fish River, commanded by Messrs. Ander-

* Crest No. 1—A Dolphin's head between wings.—R. O. Sergeant.
„ No. 2—A Bird with wings extended.—
„ No. 3—A Griffin's head betweeen wings (F. R. M. C.).—Captain Crozier.
„ No. 4—A Dove with the olive branch, (motto : " *Spero Meliora.*")—J. W. Fairholme.
„ No. 5—A Fish's head between sprigs.—Franklin family.

1. Harry D. S. Goodsir (Surgeon, *Erebus*); 2. Alex. Mc.Donald (Surgeon, *Terror*); 3. Gillies A. Macbean (Master, *Terror*); 4. John S. Peddie (Surgeon, *Terror*); 5. Sir John Franklin.

son and Stewart. They found traces proving that
some of the expedition had been on Montreal Island,
Point Ogle, and different parts of the coast at the
mouth of the Fish River, but no records or bodies
were discovered. They wished to reach King William's Land, but their boats were proved to be unequal
to the task.

There was still one expedition searching the dreary
regions of the north ;—a second American one, under
Dr. Kane, which left New York on the 30th May,
1853. These enterprising mariners forced a passage
from Baffin's Bay, directly northward (through
Smith's Sound), into the open Polar Sea.

Their great exertions, however, together with the
hardships they had endured, compelled them, on
reaching the shore of that great sea which has never
yet been sailed upon, to return.

This expedition encountered the greatest perils
and privations the human frame is capable of sus-
taining. Their ship, the *Advance*, was frozen up for
twenty months before it was decided to abandon her.
At this time they were almost without food, and with
a sledge and boat journey of 1,800 miles before them.
During the first thirty days of this terrible journey,
which they accomplished in eighty-four days, their
daily provision consisted of six ounces of bread dust,
and a piece of frozen tallow, the size of a walnut,
per man ; during the latter part they were enabled
to kill seals, birds, &c. for their sustenance. Only
one man was lost however, and he by accident.

It was on the 6th August, 1855, they saw a solitary boatmen of Upernavik, the first civilized being they met with for upwards of two years, and from him they got a cloudy idea of what had been passing in the *big world* during their absence.

"What of America?" was naturally our first question, says Dr. Kane, to which the Greenlander could give no satisfactory answer, but seemed very anxious to ejaculate the words " *Sebastopol aint taken.*" Where and what was Sebastopol? they knew nothing of such a place; and the man proceeded to inform them (to their surprise) that France and England were leagued with the Mussulman against the Russians.

"But what of Sir John Franklin?" There we were at home again; and we then heard the conflicting statement that traces of the crews of the *Erebus* and *Terror* had been found by Dr. Rae, nearly 1,000 miles south of where we had been searching for them."

This chapter would be incomplete were I to omit the history of the *Resolute,* one of the vessels abandoned by Sir E. Belcher in Melville Sound, in May, 1854. She escaped her ice-bound fetters, and on the 10th September, 1855, (sixteen months after she was abandoned) was picked up by an American whaler in Davis' Strait, having drifted about 1,200 miles through Barrow Strait and Baffin Sea. Captain Buddington, who discovered the *Resolute,* boarded her with eleven men, leaving his own bark in charge

H

of the second mate, and made the best of his way towards New York with his prize. About the middle of October, having just cleared the ice, the British bark *Albert* hove in sight, and on being signalled came alongside the *Resolute*. The news of the recovery was communicated to Captain Stuart of the · British bark, and a pair of Captain Kellet's epaulettes, found on board the abandoned vessel, were intrusted to him by Captain Buddington, with instructions to forward them to the owner.

The appearance of things on board, as represented by Captain Buddington, when he had leisure to examine the vessel, was doleful in the extreme. The cabin was strewed with books, clothing, preserved meats interspersed here and there with lumps of ice. There was one thing, however, which struck Captain Buddington as being very remarkable, and for which probably no satisfactory explanation can be given; and this was the presence of ice for several feet in thickness on the larboard side, while there was not a particle on the starboard. The only argument that can be presented to explain this curious freak of the elements is, that the *Resolute*, lying with her head to the eastward for probably more than a month, received the direct rays of the sun on the starboard quarter, and nowhere else, and thus a daily warmth was imparted to this side of the ship, while the other side, being without this heat, became as solidified with ice as though the sun never shone on it. There was

a great lack of fuel on board, although, in the course
of the search throughout the vessel, a little coal was
discovered in the hold, but the quantity was very small
and entirely inadequate to supply the vessel more than
a week. Of provisions there was enough perhaps to
last a crew of seventy-five men (the number originally
carried by the *Resolute)* for nine months. The salt
meats were the only articles that were at all in a state
of preservation. Everything had gone to decay.
Even the ship's sails found between decks were so
rotten that the sailors could thrust their fingers
through them like so much brown paper. An attempt
was subsequently made to rig a topmast studding sail
out of some of the canvas found saturated with water;
but it blew out of the gearing, and was scattered to
the winds like chaff. The lower hold was found to
contain the library of one of the officers of the expedition, valued at more than £200. The books were
entirely valueless when discovered by Captain Buddington, and subsequently thrown overboard as worth-
less rubbish.

Short handed, poorly rigged, and unfitted for the
voyage as the *Resolute* was, Captain Buddington found
it no easy task to bring the ship into port. He termi-
nated his difficult voyage, however, on the 24th
December.

On the part of the American Congress, a very
graceful act followed. It was resolved by the Senate
and House of Representatives to appropriate a sum of
40,000 dollars to the purchase of the *Resolute*, with all

the armament, equipment, and property on board. This done, the ship was moved into one of the navy yards of the United States, and there fully repaired and equipped, and then despatched to England as an offering of goodwill and friendship from the United States to Great Britain. On the 13th of November, the *Resolute*, commanded by Captain Hartstein, commenced her homeward voyage, and on the 12th of December she reached Spithead. She arrived under American colours, but as soon as she let go her anchors, the English was run up alongside of the American ensign. Every care had been taken that ingenuity could devise to replace everything on board in the same condition as when the ship was abandoned by the Arctic adventurers. The *Resolute*, indeed, is, in all probability, as sound and seaworthy in every respect as when she sailed in 1852 from the British shores upon her last Polar adventure.

The Queen and Prince Albert visited the ship, and, on being presented to the Queen, Captain Hartstein addressed her as follows:—" Allow me to welcome your Majesty on board the *Resolute*, and, in obedience to the will of my countrymen and of the President of the United States, to restore her to you, not only as an evidence of a friendly feeling to your sovereignty, but as a token of love, admiration, and respect to your Majesty personally."

The Queen seemed touched by the manly simplicity of this frank and sailor-like address, and replied, with a gracious smile, " I thank you, sir."

The royal party then went over the ship and examined her with manifest interest.

In the course of explaining the chart to Prince Albert, the latter remarked that Lady Franklin was very desirous of another expedition going out, to which Captain Hartstein replied, " That it did not surprise him, for he thought it very possible that Franklin or some of his companions might still be alive among the Esquimaux."

Captain Hartstein was invited by the Queen to dine and to spend the night at Osborne; and all the officers were permitted to visit the palace and grounds, a privilege of which they availed themselves. Among the stores found in the *Resolute* were several puncheons of fine old rum, which had been put on board in prime condition on her leaving Woolwich for the Arctic regions. One of these puncheons was sent by Captain Hartstein to Prince Albert as a relic.

The *Resolute* was visited during her stay at Portsmouth by Lady Franklin and her niece, and by Capt. M'Clintock, Capt. Sadler, Capt. Richards, Lieut. Pim, and other Arctic explorers. On Christmas-day the whole of the crew who brought her over were regaled with an excellent dinner at the George Hotel, at the expense of the British Government.

Having fulfilled the kindly mission on which they had been sent, Captain Hartstein, his officers, and crew, left on their return for the United States, in the American steamer *Washington*, from Southampton, highly delighted with their reception.

PART III.

———

"After the nation's treasure failed,
The widow's mite prevailed."

CAPT. COLLINSON.

*Lady Franklin—Voyage of the "Fox"—Discovery of
the Record and Relics—Conclusion.*

All ideas of a further search were now given up;
but there was still one who "hoped against hope,"
who knew that the great tidal line which separates the
waters of the Atlantic from those of the Pacific had
not been searched, and who, therefore, in 1857, dispatched Captain M'Clintock in the *Fox*, with every
convenience for that purpose.

"All, I am sure, must have felt the deepest sympathy
and admiration of the zeal, perseverance, and conjugal
affection displayed in the noble and untiring efforts of
Lady Franklin to relieve or discover the fate of her
distinguished husband and the gallant party under
his command.

"The name of the present Lady Franklin is as
'familiar as a household word' in every bosom in
England; she is alike the object of our admiration,
our sympathy, our hopes, and our prayers. Nay, her
name and that of her husband is breathed in prayer

in many lands—and, oh! how earnest, how zealous,
how courageous, have been her efforts to find and
relieve her husband, for, like Desdemona,

> "She loved him for the dangers he had passed,
> • And he loved her that she did pity them."

" How has she traversed from port to port, bidding
'God speed their mission' to each public and
private ship going forth on the noble errand of mercy
—how freely and promptly has she contributed to
their comforts. How has she watched each arrival
from the north, scanned each stray paragraph of news,
hurried to the Admiralty on each rumour, and kept
up with unremitting labour a voluminous corres-
pondence with all the quarters of the globe, fondly
wishing that she had the wings of the dove, that she
might flee away, and be with him from whom Heaven
has seen fit to separate her so long."*

The following is a portion of the letter of instructions Lady Franklin delivered to M'Clintock on his
departure :—" As to the objects of the expedition and
their relative importance, I am sure you know that
the rescue of any possible survivor of the *Erebus* and
Terror would be to me, as it would be to you, the
noblest result of our efforts. To this object I wish
every other to be subordinate ; and next to it in
importance is the recovery of the unspeakably precious documents of the expedition, public and private,
and the personal relics of my dear husband and his

* Simmonds.

companions. And lastly, I trust it will be in your power to confirm, directly or inferentially, the claims of my husband's expedition to the earliest discovery of the North-West Passage, which, if Dr. Rae's report be true, (and the Government of our country has accepted and rewarded it as such) these martyrs in a noble cause achieved, at their last extremity, after five long years of labour and suffering, if not at an earlier period."

Noble-minded woman! next to her husband's personal safety, his fame was the object she specially wished to declare; and in this she was well rewarded, for Franklin and his followers were "THE FIRST DISCOVERERS OF THE NORTH-WEST PASSAGE."

The *Fox* sailed from Aberdeen on the 1st of July, 1857, and arrived off Cape Farewell, on the south coast of Greenland, on the 12th. They had a favourable passage along the coast of Greenland, until they arrived in Melville Bay, where, on the 17th August, they were beset in the ice. The ice in which the *Fox* was beset, is called a *floe*, that is, an immense field of ice, the extent of which can be distinguished; it does not join the land, and consequently does not remain stationary. The floe in which they were imprisoned made a most extraordinary drift, for when it broke up, and the vessel was released (on the 23rd April, 1858), they found themselves in the southern part of Davis Strait,—not a fortnight's voyage from home. In escaping from the drift their preservation

was very miraculous : the little *Fox* was driven help-
lessly about, and sustained the most violent shocks
from the broken floe and loose icebergs. But, in the
words of Dibdin,

> " They say there's a Providence sits up aloft,
> To keep watch for the life of Poor Jack."

" The ark, which bore the hopes of a loving wife,
and the prayers of so many friends, was not to be
swallowed up in the wreck-strewn depths of Baffin's
Bay."* During this long winter, while being carried
a distance of 1,200 miles, without light or natural
heat, their life must have been very dreary. Captain
Allen Young, writing in the " CORNHILL," says : " If
any one doubt how necessary light is for our existence,
just let him shut himself up for three months in the
coal-cellar, with an underground passage into the
ice-house, where he may go for change of air, and see
if he will be in as good health and spirits at the end
of the experiment as before. At all events, he will
have obtained the best idea one can form at home of
an arctic winter in a small vessel, save that the temperature of the Arctic ice-house is —40° instead of
+32° as at home; only 72° difference ! "

A school was established by Dr. Walker for the instruction of the men, Captain M'Clintock himself
often superintending, and teaching the sailors the art
of navigation. Nor were they lost for amusements.
On the 5th November they made a Guy Fawkes,
carried him in procession round the ship, and afterwards burnt him on the floe.

At Christmas they were very merry. They had hams, plum-puddings, preserved gooseberries and apples, nuts, sweetmeats, and Burton Ale. They decorated the decks with flags, and ornamental devices of all descriptions, and at night invited Capt. M'Clintock and the officers to join them in singing songs, drinking healths, &c., and that gallant officer writes that though they were not restricted in their allowance of spirits, "amid this festivity, all were perfectly sober." New Year's Day was also observed. Capt. M'Clintock writes in his journal: "Exactly at midnight, on the 31st December, the arrival of the New Year was announced to me by our band—two flutes and an accordion—striking up at my door. There was also a procession, or perhaps I should say, a continuation of the band, these performers were grotesquely attired, and armed with frying-pans, gridirons, kettles, pots, and pans, with which to join in and add to the effect of the *other* music."

When they were released from the ice in April they made for Holsteinborg, in Greenland, where they had a refit, despatched letters to England, and received some luxuries by the way of late newspapers. They started once more, but in June had a narrow escape of being wrecked, the vessel running on a reef of unknown rocks at a spot called Buchan Island. She floated, however, with the arrival of the high tide, and got off safe.

They first made for Pond's Inlet, where Captain M'Clintock had communication with the natives;

but he obtained no information relative to those he sought. They then sailed into Barrow Strait, arriving at Beechey Island in August; here they erected a tablet, sent out by Lady Franklin, to the memory of the martyrs of the *Erebus* and *Terror*. Capt. M'Clintock also took the letters which had been left for Sir John Franklin and Capt. Collinson. Beechey Island has now quite the appearance of a colony. There is a large store-house containing all kinds of clothing, provisions, &c.; a great quantity of coal, and a number of boats. There is also a pillar, called a post office, where most of the officers visiting these regions deposit a record of their proceedings; Bellot's and Franklin's monuments, and a number of seamen's graves and head-stones or boards.*

Leaving Beechey Island they proceeded a short distance down Peel Sound, when they were obliged to return, the ice being in one solid body from shore to shore. They then made for Regent's Inlet, which fortunately was clear of ice, and steaming down it, arrived in a very short time in Brentford Bay. They then steamed through Bellot Strait, the *Fox* being the first vessel to accomplish that feat, it having been discovered and traversed by Mr. Kennedy and Lieut. Bellot in sledges. Finding no good shelter on the western side of the strait, they returned to the east, and took up their quarters for the winter in a snug harbour, named by M'Clintock Port Kennedy. In February, 1859, parties were dispatched to the

* See Appendix No. 5.

western coast of Boothia, and other parts, to deposit provisions for the coming spring journies.

During one of these excursions, Capt. M'Clintock fell in with a party of Esquimaux who gave him the information that "several years ago a ship was crushed by the ice off the north shore of King William's Land, but that all her people landed safely, and went away to the Great Fish River, where they died."

This tribe had been visited by Sir John Ross, in 1830, and many of them remembered him. Captain M'Clintock inquired after an individual (much spoken of in Ross' narrative) by name "Tulluachiu," who having lost his leg in an encounter with a bear, was supplied with a wooden one by Ross' carpenter. We are told he was not long in making good use of his new member, and the rest of the tribe were so delighted with it that many of them came to Ross begging for the same privilege.

The daughter of Tulluachiu was pointed out to M'Clintock, that being the only answer he received to his inquiry, and Mr. Petersen, the interpreter, explained that the interesting individual in question must have left this world, as they never like to speak of the dead.

In April the real searching commenced. Captain M'Clintock and his party of five men were absent from the ship 79 days, during which they travelled a distance of 910 miles, closely examining the shores of King William's Island, Montreal Island, and the mouth of the Great Fish River. By the 8th May they had obtained many interesting relics of our lost countrymen,—six silver spoons and forks, the property of Sir John Franklin and other officers,* a medal, portion of a gold watch chain, and a great quantity of wood and iron, being received from the Esquimaux near the Magnetic Pole; and six other pieces of plate bearing crests and initials of the lost officers, a number of buttons, and a quantity of wood and iron from a tribe at Cape Norton. These articles were purchased from them at the rate of four needles each. They also learned that a second ship had been seen off King William's Land, and that she drifted ashore in the fall of the same year. The natives at Cape Norton stated that the wreck had been used by them for fire-wood, but they had not visited it since 1857. They also stated that when the vessel drifted on shore there was one body in it,—a man with very large teeth.

On the 24th May, a few miles eastward of Cape Herschel, Captain M'Clintock came upon a human skeleton, the face buried in the snow. He, apparently, had been a young man, and by the fragments of dress, was an officer's servant or steward; and lying on and about him was found a clothes brush, a comb, a half-sovereign (date 1844), a sixpence (date 1831), and a pocket-book containing letters and the song of "The Sea," but nothing by which he could be recognized.

The cairn erected by Simpson at Cape Herschel,

* See Appendix No. 4.

in 1839, was examined on the 25th, and by the appearance of it Captain M'Clintock is of opinion that records were deposited there by the retreating crews of the *Erebus* and *Terror*, and subsequently removed by the natives.

A few miles further north M'Clintock joined his researches to those of Lieutenant Hobson, who, with his party, traced the northern and western shores of King William's Island. At Cape Felix he found three small tents, a few blankets, some clothing, and a boat's ensign in a canvass bag; and upon Point Victory (Ross' Farthest) he discovered a large cairn, in which was a tin case containing "A RECORD."

That Record is indeed a sad and touching relic of our lost friends. The paper is one of those printed forms which are served out to discovery ships for the purpose of being thrown overboard in bottles. Upon it, written by Lieutenant Gore, is the following information :—

27th May, 1847 $\left\{ \begin{array}{l} \text{H.M.S. } \textit{Erebus} \text{ and } \textit{Terror} \\ \text{Wintered in the ice in} \\ \text{Lat. 70° 5', Long. 98° 23' W.} \end{array} \right.$

Having wintered in 1846-7[*] at Beechey Island, in Lat. 74° 43' 28" N., Long. 91° 39' 15" W., after having ascended Wellington Channel to Lat. 77°, and returned by the west side of Cornwallis Island.

Sir John Franklin commanding the expedition. All well.

Party, consisting of two officers and six men, left the ships on Monday, 24th May, 1847.

GRAHAM GORE, *Lieut.*, and
C. F. DE VŒUX, *Mate.*

[*] This is evidently dated in mistake, and should be 1845-46.

Never had an arctic navigator such an amount of success in two years. They reached Lat. 77°, a point no other vessel has been able to attain, and returned by the west side of Cornwallis Island, a channel never before or since sailed through.

They wintered in 1845-6 at Beechey Island, and in the following summer sailed down Peel Sound as far as Lat. 70° 5', when they were obliged to halt for the second winter. This they appear to have passed pretty comfortably, for Graham Gore, in May, 1847, reports "All well," and the gallant Franklin commanding.

But, alas! round the margin of the paper upon which Gore wrote those words of hope and promise, another hand (that of Captain Fitzjames), had subsequently written the following :—

"25th April, 1848.—H.M. ships *Terror* and *Erebus* were deserted on the 22nd of April, 5 leagues N.N.W. of this, having been beset since 12th of September, 1846. The officers and crews consisting of 105 souls, under the command of Captain F. R. M. Crozier, landed here in Lat. 69° 37' 42", Long. 98° 41' W. This paper was found by Lieutenant Irving under the cairn supposed to have been built by Sir James Ross in 1831, four miles to the northward, where it had been deposited by the *late* Commander Gore in June, 1847.* Sir James Ross' pillar has not however been found, and the paper has been transferred to this position, which is that in which Sir James Ross' pillar was erected. Sir John Franklin died on the 11th June, 1847, and the total loss by deaths in the expedition has been to this date 9 officers and 15 men.

"JAMES FITZJAMES, Capt. H.M.S. *Erebus.*"

* That little word *late* shows us that he too, within the twelve-month, had passed away.

It is also signed in the left-hand corner by Capt. Crozier, who adds this information :—" We start to-morrow, 26th, for Back's Fish River."

In the short space of twelve months how changed had become the history of the Franklin Expedition, how changed from the cheerful " All well " of Graham Gore* :—

" Sir John Franklin died on the 11th June, 1847."

> " Him shall no worm devour, no vulture tear,
> Congeal'd to adamant his frame shall last,
> Though empires change, till time and tide be past."
>
> MONTGOMERY.

" Few can have cherished the hope that the gallant Franklin would ever be seen among us again ; and all will be gratified to learn that his last moments were clouded by no extraordinary perils or privations, but that the kindly hand of death released him from suffering before the commencement of the terrible trials which awaited his companions, but which their veteran commander was less fitted than they were to endure.† "

" In the glorious list of England's heroes the name of Sir John Franklin must ever hold a conspicuous position. It was not for him to die, like Wolfe or Nelson, with the welcome shout of victory ringing in his ears. He had not gone forth at the head of a British fleet to win a conqueror's fame in battle against England's foes. But the errand on which he went required all the daring, all the skill, and all the

* M'Clintock.   † Simmonds.

73

patience which are ever found united in a great captain.
He went out to seek what many before him had sought
in vain, and what his surviving comrades found—The
NORTH-WEST PASSAGE.*"

"The brave old man has found a not inappropriate
grave in the region which is indissolubly connected
with his early fame; for no Arctic navigator has added
more important contributions to our store of knowledge with regard to sterile shores and frozen inlets
of the north, or prosecuted his researches under difficulties more calculated to appal any but the most
valiant heart, than he who now sleeps among the icebergs in an unknown, but not an unhonoured grave.†"

We know where he died, we know the very day of
his death; and we can imagine how each rough
stalwart seaman would bend over and drop a tear on
that revered and well-loved body before they com-
mitted it to the deep. Death would chill every heart
and each one see his doom in the untimely fate of his
commander.—Untimely to those who survived, but
not so to Franklin, for he was mourned for by a nation
and honoured by a world.—And they buried him, and
raised no petty monument over his remains, for the
mightiest works of God in nature are for ever asso-
ciated with his name. The frozen seas are Franklin's
mausoleum; the tablet of his memory is written on
the North Pole.

* *The Times*, 1859.   † Simmonds.

K

The following poem appeared in a popular periodical
on the fate of Franklin becoming known in England:

"By polar seas, on lone King William's isle,
Where gracious summer ne'er was known to smile;
Where naught is heard, along the mournful shore,
Save grinding ice or falling iceberg's roar;
Nor aught of holy life draws loving breath,
But Nature slumbers on the throne of Death;
There, without wife or kindred at his side,
But ripe in years and honours, Franklin died!
 Much had he nobly done in earlier years,
With Parry, Lyon, Ross, his brave compeers,
To burst the bonds of Boreas' icy reign,
And solve the problem of the Arctic main;
And when in age, but hero to the last,
He flung once more his banner to the blast,
And boldly launch'd, he and his gallant crew,
To prove what man conceived of man could do,
How many anxious hearts pursued his way—
How many ardent prayers by night and day,
From either hemisphere, besieged Heaven's gate,
In suppliance for a man so good and great!
And when, alas! the shadows sank upon
His distant path, and hope scarce struggled on,
When, spite of searches, o'er and o'er again
Essay'd by kin and stranger, all in vain,
No answer came, but year on year went by,
Leaving his fate still in uncertainty;
Who shall describe th' alternate hopes and fears,
The agony confused of prayers and tears,
The throbbing pulse, the fever of the soul,
That followed each fresh venture to its goal!
Still, all was dark—the oracle was dumb—
No voice broke through, no ray relieved the gloom,
The pall unlifted hung; the hand of God
Seemed, as in jealousy, to bar the road,
And write, as on the wall at Babylon,

‘ Seek not to know what I will *not* have known ;
Retire in peace ; respect my mystery ;
The lives ye cherish are at rest with Me ! ’
—So spoke the tacit conscience—and the heart
Instinctive answer’d—it had done its part ;
Man acquiesced from effort and from prayer ;
All had been done that man might do, or dare—
And the two worlds desisted in despair.
   Who then, in sorrow’s last extremity,
When man’s strong heart had fail’d him, and each eye
Turn’d from the task away—when Franklin’s name
Had passed from living lips to hist’ry’s fame— ·
Who, then, when naught remained save to pluck forth
From Time’s grim jaws the secret of the North,
Force from the grave the all that she could say,
The when, the how, his spirit pass’d away.”

                (*London Journal,* No. 769.)

“ The survivors, 105 in number, under the command of Captains Crozier and Fitzjames, started on the 26th April, 1848, for Back’s Fish River.” On their maps, Point Victory, the spot where they landed, and also Cape Herschel and the Fish River, were designated, but the intervening territory was to them entirely unknown. Such were the circumstances under which they started on their death-march, a distance of 220 miles, in utter ignorance, not only of precise geographical details, but also of the general character of the country.

Only one person of the entire company had any previous knowledge of the locality upon which they were thrown; that was Mr. Blanky, the ice-master of the *Terror,* who, with Sir James Ross, had discovered it; but as there were nine officers dead, it is quite possible he was one of them, and if so, they were all total strangers on King William's Land.

In addition to this record, Lieutenant Hobson found at Point Victory a number of relics, including a sextant (Frederick Hornby, R.N.), the top of a gun case (C. H. Osmer, R.N.), four sets of boat cooking apparatus complete, and a medicine chest, containing the following :—

" One bottle labelled zinzib R. pulv., full; do. spirit rect., empty; do. mur. hydrarg, seven-eighths full; do. ol. cary-phyll., one-fifth full; do. ipec. P. eo., full; do. ol. menth. pip., empty; do. liq. ammon. fort., three-quarters full; do. ol. oliv., full; do. tinct. opii. camph., three-quarters full; do. vin. sem. colch., full; do. do. quarter full; do. calomel, full (broken); do. hydrarg. nit. oxyd., full; do. pulv. Gregor, full (broken); do. magnes. carb., full; do. camphor, full; two bottles tinct. tolu. (each) quarter full; one bottle ipec. R. pulv. full; do. jalap R. pulv. full; do. scammon pulv., full; do. quina. bisulph., empty; do. (not labelled) tinct. opii, three-quarters full; one box (apparently) purgative pills, full; do. ointment, shrunk; do. omp. adhesiv., full; one probang, one pen wrapped up in lint, one lead pencil, one pewter syringe, two small tubes (test) wrapped up in lint, one farthing, bandages, oil silk, lint, and thread."

Proceeding in a south-westerly direction, in Lat. 69° 09′ N., and Long. 99° 27′ W., Hobson discovered a piece of wood sticking out of the snow, and on digging round it a boat was discovered. In this boat were two human skeletons: one, apparently a young man of slender proportions, and, by some fragments of clothing, supposed to be an officer; the other a large and strong man. One, in the bottom of the stern sheets, was covered with a great quantity of thrown-off clothing; the other, in the bows, appeared to have been that of some poor fellow who had crept there to look out, and, in that position, fallen into his long last sleep.

In this boat was found the chronometers of both ships; five watches; twenty-six pieces of silver plate (all bearing the names of some of the lost officers); a small prayer-book; cover of a small book of " Family Prayers; " " Christian Melodies, " an inscription within the cover to " G. G." (Graham Gore?); " The Vicar of Wakefield; " a New Testament in the French language; and a small Bible, interlined in many places, and with numerous references written in the margin.

> " Most wondrous book! bright candle of the Lord!
> Star of eternity! the only star
> By which the bark of man could navigate
> The sea of life, and gain the coast of bliss securely."

What wonderful mystery hangs over the few volumes which were thus found with the lost mariners ! They being, with one exception, all of a religious character, intimate from what source the abandoned heroes sought for comfort and support

when every prospect of success was shut out. As in
death one might turn towards a friend's face to seek
in its expression some sympathy or comfort, so these
perishing and forlorn men sought in the pages of their
treasured volumes a ray of hope and happiness beyond
the world of snow and ice in which they were imprisoned.

' "And though all this be come upon us, yet do we not forget
thee: nor behave ourselves frowardly in thy covenant.
"No, not when thou hast smitten us, and covered us with
the shadow of death." (PSALM XLIV.)

In this boat was also found a quantity of ammunition, tea, and chocolate, and a number of articles
required for common use. Two double-barrelled guns
—one barrel in each being loaded—stood upright
against the side of the boat, precisely as they had
been placed eleven years previously.

All these relics are now to be seen in the United
Service Institution, grouped in a most beautiful yet
melancholy manner. The Bible lies open at that
most beautiful 15th chapter of St. Paul's Corinthians,
in which doubtless these brave men read that their
failing, perishing bodies, together with their immortal
souls, should survive that terrible ordeal, and rise
again in glorious incorruption. The two guns lie on
the table marked "loaded," by the fingers which were
soon to be rigid with a yet more frozen coldness than
that of the icy seas.

I would entreat everyone to visit these memorials;

for while, perhaps, the sight of them would raise a sad feeling in their breasts, they would experience a sensation of happiness at having seen all that remains of their dear lost countrymen, and of having paid the only possible tribute to their memory.

The discovery of the skeletons by Capt. M'Clintock verifies the assertion of the Esquimaux:—that exhausted by scurvy and starvation, they "dropped as they walked along."

One old woman told Dr. Rae that a party of her tribe arrived at Montreal Island, while one of the white men remained alive, but they were too late to render any assistance. Her speech was:—"I saw him die; he was large and strong; he sat on the sandy beach, his face rested on his hands." Let us for a moment picture to ourselves the despair and misery of this poor soul when the fearful truth flashed upon him that he was alone in the awful solitude. Doubtless he called wildly on God to restore to him the dead, or to take his life: it is easy to conjecture that reason would forsake him, that he would rave of home, and people the horrid waste with familiar faces; that the scene would change, and he would behold his beloved commander and his lost comrades, that he would utter a cry which might bring pity into the heart of a savage beast; and, at last, faint and broken-hearted, he would sink and die: but "though his body was a frozen corpse his spirit was in Paradise."

"Alas!
Nor wife, nor children, more shall he behold;
Nor friends, nor sacred home. On every nerve
The deadly Winter seizes; shuts up sense;
And, o'er his inmost vitals creeping cold,
Lays him along the snows, a stiffen'd corse!
Stretch'd out, and bleaching in the northern blast."
THOMSON.

"I looked on my right hand, and beheld, but there was no man that would know me: refuge failed me." (PSALM CXLII.)

"Our bones are scattered at the grave's mouth, like as when one cutteth and cleaveth wood upon the earth.

"But mine eyes are unto thee, O God the Lord: in thee is my trust; leave not my soul destitute." (PSALM CXLI.)

"They all perished, and in dying in the cause of their country, their dearest consolation must have been to feel that Englishmen would not rest until they had followed up their footsteps, and had given to the world what they could not then give—the grand result of their dreadful voyage—their discovery of the NORTH-WEST PASSAGE. They had sailed down Peel and Victoria Straits, now appropriately named Franklin Straits, and the poor human skeletons lying upon the shores of the waters in which Dease and Simpson had sailed from the westward, bore melancholy evidence of their success.*"

By the end of June, all the searching parties were again safe on board the *Fox*. Captain Allen Young, though he was not fortunate enough to find any traces of our countrymen, filled up the coast lines of North Somerset and Prince of Wales Land, proving the

* Cornhill Magazine.

latter to be an island. He was absent from the ship twice—the first time travelling 630 miles in 62 days; and the second, 310 miles in 19 days, and during part of this time had but one man for a companion.

Mr. Brand, the engineer, and Scott, the engine driver, both died during the voyage, so Captain M'Clintock, with the assistance of the stokers, got the engines in order, and drove them himself. They left Port Kennedy on the 8th August, and on the 20th September arrived in England.

Before concluding, I must not omit to say a few words about Captain Sir Leopold M'Clintock. A man better fitted for the errand on which he was sent did not exist. It is not a great navigator who is required in these seas so much as a kind, patient, and generous man ; one who will exert himself to the utmost to cheer his men, and by his example cause them to think lightly of the great hardships they have to endure. M'Clintock is one of these. He had served in three previous searching expeditions— Sir James Ross', in 1849 ; Admiral Austin's, in 1851 ; and Sir Edward Belcher's, in 1853-4, and had always made it his study to endeavour to lighten the loads of sledge-parties, and to promote the comfort of his men in every possible manner.

It is not well known (indeed M'Clintock's foot-note at page 403 of his work is even calculated to mislead) that he and Captain Allen Young refused to accept of any pay from Lady Franklin for their

L

services, and that Young in addition contributed £500 from his private resources towards the outfit of the expedition.

Francis Leopold M'Clintock was born at Dundalk, in Ireland, in 1819, and entered the Navy in June, 1831.

NOTE.—Mrs. Gell, the only child of the late Sir John Franklin, died during the first week in September, 1860 (since the note at page 36 of this work was printed.)

The Rev. Mr. Gell is, at present, incumbent of St. John's, Notting Hill.

CONCLUSION.

"This is a sad but glorious tale. It is sad to think that we have lost so many brave men; that far away, amid frost and snow, in the dark inhospitable north, heroic Englishmen have given up their precious lives —a costly sacrifice to science. And yet a gleam of pride lights up our sorrow, for all England delights to hold in honour the memory of those who have given to the world such an example of energy and enterprise. It is not without a sense of relief that we welcome back Captain M'Clintock and his gallant companions. We now feel that our duty in this matter is accomplished—that the truth is known, and the last sacrifice made.*"

"Very little more will probably have to be added to the scroll of Arctic discovery.—The chart of the Arctic regions is no longer a blank; we have at least filled up the coast outlines of the American continent and its adjacent straits and bays; and thus much has been gained for Science, although at a heavy outlay and fearful risk.

* *The Times*, 1859.

"The cost of the various Government Arctic Expeditions up to the time of the outfit of Sir John Franklin's vessels, amounted to £336,317. The outlay since incurred for the various searching expeditions by land and sea has been about £900,000.

"The sad fate of Sir John Franklin and his gallant companions has thrown a gloom on the subject, but it ought to be remembered that, up to the present period, our successive Polar voyages have, without exception, given occupation to the energies and gallantry of British seamen, and have extended the realms of magnetic and general science, at an expense of lives and money quite insignificant, compared with the ordinary dangers and casualties of such expeditions, and that it must be a very narrow spirit and view of the subject which can raise the cry of *" Cui bono,"* and counsel us to relinquish the honour and peril of such enterprises to Russia and the United States of America.* "

" One touch of Nature makes the whole world kin."

During the last twelve years, the civilized, and even some of the barbarous, nations have deeply sympathised in our great bereavement, and many have stretched out a helping hand in the attempts to recover the lost.

Political and national divergences were made of no account. Over against them stood the telling fact that a portion of God's family, astray upon the earth,

* Simmonds.

was to be sought out and rescued. The call came in that " powerful language, to no realm or region confined;

> ——Nature's voice, and understood
> Alike by all mankind."

" From the east and from the west, from the north and from the south," came in affectionate responses to the silent appeal of Britain, and her noble widowed daughter.

Our inland German cousins were necessarily unable to offer active service in a nautical expedition,—yet they too came forward,—the illustrious Humboldt in their van,—with sentiments expressive of their hearts' interest in the scheme, and propositions as to its conduct which proved of great value. France contributed Debrae, and Bellot, a martyr to the cause. Russia left unexplored no part of the Polar Sea adjoining her own vast territory; while the Danes not only dispatched Petersen, who acted as interpreter to nearly all the expeditions, from Austin's to M'Clintock's, inclusive; but at all times manifested the greatest possible kindness to any of our mariners who approached their colony. Of our noble kinsmen beyond the Atlantic, it is impossible to say too much. They not only expended considerable sums of money, but engaged *themselves*, in their own vessels, in an anxious and laborious search.

The issue has been already told :—Of all that left us fifteen years ago, with brave hearts and gallant hopes, there remains but whitened bones upon the desolate ice-plains of the North. And yet, not altogether thus ;—for there rests in our memory the proof of the existence of a bond of brotherhood soon admitted when much demanded.

And while many have contributed their gallant efforts in the cause of God, of humanity, and of the noblest and most devoted of British women, conspicuous on the rolls of this memorable history of the ill-fated expedition, as greater among lesser stars, are the names of Bellot, of Kane, and of Grinnel ; while the whole history of gallant enterprise and touching self-denial furnishes irresistible evidence of the truth of the poet's sentiment, that there is

> " No land but listens to the common call.
> . . . .
> The genial intercourse, and mutual aid,
> Cheer what were else a universal shade."

APPENDIX No. 1.

LIST OF CELEBRATED ARCTIC DISCOVERERS.

DATE.	NAMES.	DISCOVERIES.	REMARKS.
1553.	Sir Hugh Willoughby	Nova Zembla	Perished, 1554.*
1553.	Richard Chancellor	White Sea, Archangel, &c.	Perished, 1556.*
1576.	Sir Martin Frobisher	Frobisher's Strait	Killed, 1594.
1578.	*Gaspar de Cortereal*	} (Brothers). Straits of Gaspar, &c.	Fate unknown.
1579.	*Michael de Cortereal*		
1585.	John Davis	Davis's Strait, &c.	Killed, 1605.
1594.	*William Barentz*	Spitzbergen	Perished, 1594-5.
1610.	Sir Henry Hudson	Hudson's Bay	Fate unknown.
1616.	William Baffin	Baffin's Sea, &c.	Killed, 1622.
1722.	*Vitus Behring*	Behring's Strait	Shipwrecked and died on Behring Island, 1741.
1776.	James Cook	Through Behring's Strait to Icy Cape	Killed, 1779.
1818-30.	Sir John Ross	Booothia, &c.	Died, 1856.
1819-27.	Sir Edward Parry	Parry Islands, &c., &c.	Died, 1855.
1819-45.	Sir John Franklin	Northern Coast of America	{ Died on board the *Erebus*, 1847.
1833.	Sir George Back	Fish River, &c.	{ Received £5,000 and the order of knighthood.
1850.	Sir Robert M'Clure	THE NORTH-WEST PASSAGE	
1853.	*Dr. Kane*	Kennedy Channel, Kane Sea, &c.	Died, 1857.
1850-59.	Sir Leopold M'Clintock	Prince Patrick Island, &c., &c., &c.	{ Received the order of knighthood for discovering the "only authentic" information relative to the Franklin expedition.

Other Arctic discoverers of the 16th, 17th, and 18th centuries, were Burrogh, Mercator, Pet, Jackman, Sir Humphrey Gilbert, Poole, Sir Thomas Button, James Hall (killed by an Esquimaux), Luke Fox, James, Middleton, Hearne, Mackenzie, Duncan, and *Kotzebue*. And of the present century : Buchan, Lyon, Sir James Ross, Dease, Simpson, Rae, Austin, Collinson, *De Haven*, Osborn, Browne, Kellett, and Kennedy.

Note.—All were English, excepting those whose names are in italics.

APPENDIX No. 2.

THE NORTH-EAST PASSAGE.

So far back as the days of Edward VI there was formed the general plan of a voyage, the object of which was to reach the far-famed regions of India and Cathay, by the way of the north and north-east. The first expedition which sailed on this enterprise consisted of three vessels, under the command of Sir Hugh Willoughby:—the *Bona Speranza*, 120 tons (Willoughby); the *Edward Bonaventura*, 160 tons (Chancellor); and the *Bona Confidentia*, 90 tons, which were fitted out by the "Mystery and Company of Merchants Adventurers for the Discovery of Regions, Dominions, Islands, and places unknown," whose governor was Sebastian Cabot.

Cabot, the Grand Pilot of England, prepared a series of instructions for the guidance of the crews of these vessels, and among them was one which enjoined that "morning and evening prayers were to be read on board each ship by the chaplain or master;" and it was ordered that there should be no "ribaldry or ungodly talk; dicing, carding, or other devilish games."

"Conspiracies, part-takings, factions, false tales, which be the very seeds and fruits of contention," were expressly forbidden; and the "strange peoples" visited were to be considered "advisedly, and treated with gentleness and courtesy, without any disdain, laughing, or contempt." They were to use all possible fair means to decoy a native of any new found "countrie," on board their ship, and he was to be well clothed and treated; and, adds the Grand Pilot—"If he be made drunk by your wine or beer, you shall know the secrets of his heart."

This latter intimation is unworthy of a place in the preceding instructions, and shows the depravity which at that time existed, even in the minds of the higher classes.

On the 10th May, 1553, this expedition took its departure from Deptford. Early in the morning they dropped down to Greenwich, where, at that time, was the court. The youthful monarch was prevented by illness from gazing on the spectacle; but the chief courtiers were at the windows of the palace; the rest of the household occupied the houses, while crowds of people lined the shore. The ships fired their guns, and the welkin rang with the shouts of the mariners, while great was the exultation of all around. On proceeding to the Essex coast, and then to Gravesend, the three vessels were detained for a few days, by contrary winds; but a propitious gale springing up, they directed their course into the expanse of the German Sea.

In the following year, the *Edward Bonaventura*, commanded by Richard Chancellor, returned alone to England, having been separated from the other vessels, by a gale, in the preceding July. Chancellor had discovered the White Sea, and wintered in it, and was there very kindly treated by the Russians, who, at that time, were but imperfectly known. He effected a treaty of commerce with Ivan Valisovitch, the potentate of Archangel; and, through him, with the Muscovite sovereign. This treaty was warmly welcomed in England, and a number of traders were collected in a very short time, who assumed the title of the "Muscovy Company."

In 1557 Stephen Burrough was dispatched in search of Sir Hugh Willoughby, and the two vessels under his command. At Kegor, he learned from a Drontheim skipper that the *Bona Confidentia* was lost, and he had bought her sails for his ship, but of the other vessel he could obtain no intelligence. It was afterwards ascertained, from a party of Russians, that the *Bona Speranza* had been discovered frozen in a bay in the north of Lapland, in the spring of 1554; and the frozen bodies of the crew were all on board. The Russians also delivered up all the papers belonging to the vessel, by which it was ascertained they entered this "harbour of death" on the 18th September, and remained a week before resolving to winter there; and they sent out three exploring parties, two of which appear to have been absent from the ship, at least, six, and one, eight days. This brings them to the middle of October, where the journal suddenly ceased; but another paper proves that some of the party were alive in January, 1554.

Chancellor was again sent to Russia by the Muscovy Company; but on returning, his vessel was wrecked off the coast of Scotland, and he, with the greater part of his crew, perished.

The Dutch, in 1594, dispatched an expedition to the North, under the command of William Barentz, a nautical man of no ordinary ability. He made two subsequent voyages, in the last, discovering Spitzbergen, where he died.

The coast outlines of Northern Asia were filled up by the Russians, in the early part of the last century.

APPENDIX No. 3.

LIST OF THE OFFICERS OF THE EREBUS AND TERROR,

WITH THEIR PREVIOUS SERVICES.

EREBUS.

CAPTAIN SIR JOHN FRANKLIN.—See page 32.

COMMANDER JAMES FITZJAMES.—Entered the Navy on the
25th of August, 1825. Served in the Gulf of Mexico; Mediterranean (during the Greek Revolution); Col. Chesney's
Euphrates Expedition (where he was taken prisoner by a
tribe of Bedouin Arabs); Syrian War (1840); China War
(wounded); Coast of Africa.

LIEUTENANT GRAHAM GORE.—Entered the Navy on the 27th
April, 1820. Served at the Battle of Navarino; Capture of
Aden; Back's voyage in the *Terror*; China; East Indies.

LIEUTENANT HENRY THOMAS DUNDAS LE VESCONTE.—Entered
the Navy on the 19th May, 1829. Served in the China War
(greatly distinguished himself on three occasions, his name
each time being honorably mentioned); East Indies; Coast
of Africa; Channel.

LIEUTENANT JAMES WALTER FAIRHOLME.—Entered the Navy
on the 12th March, 1834. Served in the West Indies; Coast
of Africa (where he was wrecked and taken prisoner by
the Moors); Syrian War; Niger Expedition.

LIEUTENANT CHARLES F. DES VŒUX.—First Voyage.

LIEUTENANT ROBERT ORME SERGEANT.—First Voyage.

LIEUTENANT E. COUCH.

Master—HENRY F. COLLINS.

Ice-Master—JAMES REID.

Purser—CHARLES H. OSMER.

Surgeon—STEPHEN S. STANLEY,

    „ —HARRY D. GOODSIR.

Clerk—G. F. PINHORN,

TERROR.

CAPTAIN FRANCIS RAWDON MOIRA CROZIER.—Born at Banbridge, Ireland. Entered the Navy on the 10th June, 1810. Served in the Pacific; Cape of Good Hope; Arctic (with Parry in 1821-24-27); Spain and Portugal; Baffin's Bay (in search of some missing whalers); Antarctic Expedition (1839-43).

LIEUTENANT EDWARD LITTLE. — Mediterranean; South America.

LIEUTENANT GEORGE HENRY HODGSON.—Entered the Navy on the 14th June, 1832. Served on the Coast of Portugal; South America; Mediterranean; China War (particularly distinguished himself); Engagement with Pirates on the Pedir Coast; Channel.

LIEUTENANT JOHN IRVING.—Entered the Navy on the 25th June, 1828. Served in the East Indies; North America; West Indies.

LIEUTENANT FREDERICK J. HORNBY.—Mediterranean; West Indies.

LIEUTENANT ROBERT THOMAS.—First Voyage.

Master—GILLIES A. MACBEAN.

Ice-Master—THOMAS BLANKY.

Surgeon—JOHN SMART PEDDIE.

    „ —ALEXANDER MCDONALD.

Clerk—EDWIN J. HELPMAN.

APPENDIX No. 4.

List of Individuals of the Franklin Expedition of whom satisfactory accounts have been received ; also of those of whom relics have been found.

Sir John Franklin *(Erebus)*.—Died 11th June, 1847.

Commander Graham Gore *(Erebus)*.—Died between June, 1847, and April, 1848.

Seamen—John Hartnell *(Erebus)*.—Died January 4th, 1846.

    „   John Torrington *(Terror)*.—Died Jan. 1st, 1846.

    „   James Elliott *(Terror)*
    „   Thomas Birt *(Erebus)*
    „   Robert Carr *(Terror)*   } Invalided home from Greenland, 1845.
    „   William Brown *(Terror)*
Marine—William Aitken *(Terror)*
    „   William Braine *(Erebus)*—Died April 3rd, 1846.

RELICS FOUND.

A quantity of Plate, and Guelphic Order, belonging to Sir John Franklin.

On one of Sir John Franklin's spoons is scratched " W. G." (William Goddard, *Terror*) ; and on another " W. W." (William Wentzell, *Terror*).

A number of Silver Spoons and Forks, the property of—

> Captain F. R. M. Crozier,
> Lieutenant Graham Gore,
> Lieutenant Henry Le Vesconte,
> Lieutenant James Fairholme,
> Master Gillies Macbean,
> Surgeon Henry Goodsir,
> Surgeon John Peddie.

A Silver Medal belonging to Surgeon Alexander McDonald.

A Sextant belonging to Lieutenant Frederic Hornby.

Top of a Gun Case belonging to Purser Charles Osmer.

Piece of Flannel Shirt, marked " F. D. V.", 1845 (Lieutenant C. F. des Vaux).

Tin Case, marked " Fowler," (*Erebus*).

Meat Tin, marked " W. Mark," (*Erebus*).

Knife Handle, marked " Hickey," (*Terror*).

Canteen, marked " Wm. Hedges," (marine, *Terror*).

      „   marked " Wm. Hether,"   „

Knife Handle, marked " W. R." { (William Rhodes ?) *Terror*. (William Reid ?) *Erebus*.

Piece of Stocking, marked " W. S." { (William Smith ?) *Erebus*. (William Steny ?) *Terror*. (William Sinclair ?) *Terror*.

APPENDIX No. 5.

ACCOUNT OF THE MONUMENTS, GRAVES, &C., AT
BEECHEY ISLAND.

1.—Sacred to the memory of JOHN TORRINGTON, who departed
this life January 1st, A.D. 1846, on board of Her Majesty's
ship *Terror*, aged 20 years.

2.—Sacred to the memory of JOHN HARTNELL, A.B., of Her·
Majesty's ship *Erebus;* died January 4, 1846, aged 25
years.—"Thus saith the Lord of Hosts, consider your
ways."—HAGGAI, Chap. I., v. 7.

3.—Sacred to the memory of W. BRAINE, R.M., of Her Majesty's
ship *Erebus*, who died April 3rd, 1846, aged 32 years.—
"Choose you this day whom you will serve."—JOSHUA,
Chap. II., 4th part of the 15th verse.

4.—Sacred to the memory of Mons. BELLOT, Lieutenant of the
French Navy, and Chevalier of the Legion of Honour,
who accompanied Mr. Kennedy and Capt. Inglefield, on
their respective visits to the Arctic Regions. While
attached to Her Majesty's steam-vessel *Phœnix*, under
Captain Inglefield, he gallantly volunteered to convey
despatches to Captain Sir E. Belcher, with a sledge crew
from Her Majesty's ship *North Star*. In a heavy gale
of wind, on the 18th August, 1853, he was drowned by
the disruption of the ice, near Cape Grinnell, much
lamented by the Arctic Squadron, and all who had the
pleasure of knowing his value and noble spirit.

N

5.—Sacred to the memory of WILLIAM CUTBUSH, Private, Royal Marines, of Her Majesty's ship *Assistance*, a native of Northiam, Sussex, who died on board, 27th February, 1853, after a protracted illness from disease of the lungs, aged 24 years. He served with credit in his Corps for upwards of 16 years and 4 months, gaining by his good conduct two badges of merit, in addition to the Syrian Medal. During 12 months of the above period he served in Her Majesty's ship *Assistance*, gaining the respect of captain and officers, and beloved by all who knew him, and died deeply lamented by his shipmates.—"Happy are they who die in the Lord." He lies interred in Northumberland Sound.

6.—Sacred to the memory of ISAAC BARNETT, Captain of the Maintop, and GEORGE Harris, A.B., seaman of Her Majesty's ship *Assistance*—the latter attached to Her Majesty's ship tender *Pioneer*. Isaac Barnett departed this life on 28th January, 1854, aged 28 years. George Harris departed this life on 9th January, 1854, aged 30¼ years. Both fell victims to scurvy, although the former laboured primarily under scorbutic affection of the ankle. Their remains lie interred on shore at Disaster Bay, where Her Majesty's ship *Assistance* and Tender wintered in 1853-54.—"Blessed are they that die in the Lord."

7.—Sacred to the memory of JOHN AMES, A.B., who died on board Her Majesty's ship *Investigator*, at Baring Island, April 11th, 1853, aged 29 years.

8.—Sacred to the memory of JOHN BOYLE, A.B., who died on board Her Majesty's ship *Investigator*, at Baring Island, April 6th, 1853, aged 29 years.

9.—Sacred to the memory of THOMAS MORGAN, A.B., of Her
Majesty's ship *Investigator*, who died on board Her
Majesty's ship *North Star*, at Beechey Island, May 22nd,
1854, aged 34 years.

10.—Sacred to the memory of Mr. H. H. SAINSBURY, Mate,
late of Her Majesty's ship *Investigator*, who died on board
Her Majesty's ship *Resolute*, off Cape Cockburn, November
14th, 1853, aged 26 years.

> Relieved from earthly sorrows, which on my heart hath press'd,
> I thank the gentle hand Divine which lays this heart to rest.

11.—Sacred to the memory of THOMAS MOBLEY, Private, Royal
Marines, who died suddenly on board Her Majesty's ship
Resolute, at Dealy Island, October 19th, 1852, aged 40
years. Also to the memory of GEORGE DROVER, Captain
of the Forecastle, who died on board Her Majesty's ship
tender *Intrepid*, at Dealy Island, December 12th, 1852,
aged 28 years.

12.—Sacred to the memory of JOHN COOMBES, Stoker, of Her
Majesty's ship tender *Intrepid*, who died suddenly while
travelling near Point Nias, Melville Island, May 12th,
1853, aged 34 years. Also to the memory of THOMAS
HOOD, Private, Royal Marines, who died on board Her
Majesty's ship *Intrepid*, off Cape Cockburn, January 2nd,
1854, aged 36 years.

13.—Sacred to the memory of JOHN KERR, Gunner's Mate, who
died on board Her Majesty's ship *Investigator*, at Baring
Island, April 13th, 1853, aged 34 years. Also to the
memory of JAMES WILKIE, Ice-Quartermaster, who died
on board Her Majesty's ship tender *Intrepid*, off Cape
Cockburn, February 2nd, 1854, aged 38 years.

TO THE MEMORY OF
FRANKLIN,
CROZIER, FITZJAMES,
**AND ALL THEIR
GALLANT BROTHER OFFICERS AND FAITHFUL
COMPANIONS WHO HAVE SUFFERED AND PERISHED
IN THE CAUSE OF SCIENCE AND
THE SERVICE OF THEIR COUNTRY.**

THIS TABLET
**IS ERECTED NEAR THE SPOT WHERE
THEY PASSED THEIR FIRST ARCTIC
WINTER, AND WHENCE THEY ISSUED
FORTH TO CONQUER DIFFICULTIES OR
TO DIE.**

**IT COMMEMORATES THE GRIEF OF THEIR
ADMIRING COUNTRYMEN AND FRIENDS,
AND THE ANGUISH SUBDUED BY FAITH,
OF HER WHO HAS LOST, IN THE HEROIC
LEADER OF THE EXPEDITION, THE MOST
DEVOTED AND AFECTIONATE OF
HUSBANDS.**

---

*" And so HE bringeth them unto the Haven
where they would be."*

1855.

This Stone has been intrusted to be affixed in its place by the Officers and Crew of the American Expedition, Commanded by Lieut. H. J. Hartstein, in search of Dr. Kane and his Companions.

This Tablet having been left at Disco by the American Expedition, which was unable to reach Beechey Island, in 1855, was put on board the Discovery Yacht " Fox," and is now set up here by Captain M'Clintock, R.N., commanding the final expedition of search for ascertaining the fate of Sir John Franklin and his Companions. 1858.

APPENDIX No. 6.

LIST OF THE SHIPS ENGAGED DURING THE PRESENT CENTURY IN SEARCHING OUT THE NORTH-WEST PASSAGE; ALSO THOSE ENGAGED IN SEARCHING FOR SIR JOHN FRANKLIN.

ISABELLA.—Ross.

ALEXANDER.—Parry.

DOROTHEA.—Buchan.

TRENT.—Franklin.

HECLA.—Parry — Three voyages; sold into the Merchant Service.

GRIPER.—Liddon, Lyon, and Clavering.—Three voyages; remained many years as a hulk in Chichester Harbour; broken up in 1859.

FURY.—Parry and Hoppner—Two voyages; wrecked in Regent's Inlet.

BLOSSOM.—Beechey.

VICTORY.—Ross—Abandoned in the Gulf of Boothia.

EREBUS.—Franklin—Abandoned in Franklin Strait.

TERROR.—Back and Crozier—Two voyages; abandoned in Franklin Strait.

ENTERPRISE.—Sir James Ross and Collinson—Two voyages; laid up in ordinary, Chatham.

INVESTIGATOR.—————— and M'Clure—Two voyages; abandoned in Mercy Bay.

RESOLUTE.—Austin and Kellett—Two voyages; abandoned and recovered; laid up in ordinary, Sheerness.

ASSISTANCE.—Ommaney and Belcher—Two voyages; abandoned in Melville Sound.

INTREPID.—Cator and M'Clintock—Two voyages; abandoned in Melville Sound.

PIONEER.—Osborn—Two voyages; abandoned in Melville Sound; the wreck of this vessel, or of the "Intrepid," was seen by M'Clintock in Baffin Sea.

ADVANCE.—De Haven and Kane—Two voyages; abandoned in Smith's Sea.

FOX.—M'Clintock—Presented to Sir L. M'Clintock by Lady Franklin, 1859.

PLOVER.—Moore and Maguire—Two voyages.

PRINCE ALBERT.—Forsyth and Kennedy—Two voyages; the property of Lady Franklin.

FELIX.—Ross—The property of the late Sir John Ross.

NORTH STAR,
LADY FRANKLIN,
PHŒNIX,
SOPHIA,
TALBOT,
BREADALBANE, (wrecked)

These vessels have been frequently engaged under different circumstances.

Milton Keynes UK
Ingram Content Group UK Ltd.
UKHW012033161123
432711UK00006B/433

9 781446 086582